The Art of Thomas Merton

The Art of Thomas Merton

By Ross Labrie

THE TEXAS CHRISTIAN UNIVERSITY PRESS
Fort Worth, Texas 76129

Published by the Texas Christian University Press

Library of Congress Catalog Card No. 79-1341
Manufactured in the United States of America

Library of Congress Cataloging in Publication Data

Labrie, Ross.
  The art of Thomas Merton.

  Bibliography: p.
  1. Merton, Thomas, 1915-1968 — Criticism and inter-
pretation. I. Title.
PS3525.E7174Z76   818'.5'409   79-1341
ISBN 0-912646-48-9
ISBN 0-912646-55-1 pbk.

Acknowledgements

Grateful acknowledgement is made to the trustees of the Merton Legacy Trust for permission to quote from unpublished manuscripts and letters by Thomas Merton and to quote from the Merton tapes. Copyright 1976 by the trustees of the Merton Legacy Trust and reprinted with the permission of New Directions Publishing Corp., agents.

Grateful acknowledgement is also made to the trustees of the Merton Legacy Trust and to New Directions Publishing Corp. for permission to photograph and publish pages of Merton's manuscripts: from the prologue to *The Geography of Lograire*, copyright 1968, 1969 by the trustees of the Merton Legacy Trust, reprinted with the permission of New Directions Publishing Corp.; from an early draft of *Seeds of Destruction*, copyright 1961, 1962, 1963, 1964 by the Abbey of Gethsemani, reprinted with the permission of Farrar, Straus and Giroux; from an early draft of *My Argument With the Gestapo*, copyright 1968 by Thomas Merton, copyright 1969 by the Abbey of Gethsemani, reprinted with the permission of Doubleday and Co. and from an early draft of *Conjectures of a Guilty Bystander*, copyright 1965, 1966 by the Abbey of Gethsemani, reprinted with the permission of Doubleday and Co.

Grateful acknowledgement is made to the Columbia University Library for permission to reprint excerpts from the letters of Thomas Merton to Mark Van Doren; to the trustees of the Merton Legacy Trust and to the Boston College Library for permission to reprint excerpts from an early draft of *The Seven Storey Mountain*, copyright 1948 by Harcourt, Brace, and Co.; to Yale University, James Laughlin, and New Directions Corp. for permission to quote from the letters of Thomas Merton to William Carlos Williams.

In addition, grateful acknowledgement is made to the following

the Abbey of Gethsemani; *The Secular Journal of Thomas Merton*, copyright 1959 by Madonna House; *Seeds of Destruction*, copyright 1961, 1962, 1963, 1964 by the Abbey of Gethsemani; *Thoughts in Solitude*, copyright 1956, 1958 by the Abbey of Our Lady of Gethsemani.

— to Doubleday and Co. for permission to quote from *Conjectures of a Guilty Bystander*, copyright 1965, 1966 by the Abbey of Gethsemani; *Contemplation in a World of Action*, copyright 1965, 1969, 1970, 1971 by the trustees of the Merton Legacy Trust; *My Argument With the Gestapo*, copyright 1969 by the Abbey of Gethsemani.

— to Harcourt, Brace, Jovanovich for permission to quote from *The Ascent to Truth*, copyright 1951 by the Abbey of Our Lady of Gethsemani; *No Man Is an Island*, copyright 1955 by the Abbey of Our Lady of Gethsemani; *The Seven Storey Mountain*, copyright 1948 by Harcourt, Brace, and Co.; *The Sign of Jonas*, copyright 1953 by the Abbey of Our Lady of Gethsemani; *A Thomas Merton Reader*, ed. Thomas P. McDonnell, copyright 1938, 1961, 1962 by the Abbey of Gethsemani; *The Waters of Siloe*, copyright 1949 by Rev. M. Louis (Thomas Merton).

— to Unicorn Press for permission to quote from "The Originators," *Unicorn Folio*, series one, number three, copyright 1967.

— to Notre Dame University Press for permission to quote from *Faith and Violence*, copyright 1968 by the University of Notre Dame Press.

— to the Liturgical Press for permission to quote from *Opening the Bible*, copyright 1970 by the trustees of the Merton Legacy Trust.

— to Cistercian Publications for permission to quote from *The Climate of Monastic Prayer*, copyright 1969 by the trustees of the Merton Legacy Trust.

— to Seabury Press for permission to quote from *Albert Camus's The Plague: Introduction and Commentary*, copyright 1968 by the Seabury Press.

— to Burns and Oates for permission to quote from *Redeeming the Time*, copyright 1964, 1966 by the Abbey of Gethsemani.

— to the Abbey of Gethsemani for permission to quote from *Monastic Peace*, copyright 1958 by the Abbey of Gethsemani.

Grateful acknowledgement is also made to the following:

— to Doubleday and Co. for permission to quote from Edward Rice, *The Man in the Sycamore Tree: The Good Life and Hard Times of Thomas Merton*, copyright 1970 by Edward Rice; Frederick Joseph Kelly, *Man Before God: Thomas Merton on Social Responsibility*, copyright 1974 by Frederick Joseph Kelly, S.J.; Naomi Burton, *More Than Sentinels*, copyright 1964 by Naomi Burton.

— to Herder and Herder, Inc. for permission to quote from Ernesto Cardenal, *To Live is to Love*, copyright 1972 by Herder and Herder.

— to the Dartmouth College Library for permission to quote from *Polar Notes*, number seven (Nov., 1967), copyright 1967 by Dartmouth College.

— to Sheed and Ward for permission to quote from *Thomas Merton, Monk: A Monastic Tribute*, ed. Br. Patrick Hart, copyright 1974 by the Abbey of Gethsemani; Clare Boothe Luce, ed., *Saints For Now*, copyright 1952 by Sheed and Ward.

— to Houghton-Mifflin Co. for permission to quote from John Howard Griffin, *A Hidden Wholeness: The Visual World of Thomas Merton*, copyright 1970 by John Howard Griffin.

— to New Directions Publishing Corp. for permission to quote from Nicanor Parra, *Poems and Antipoems*, intr. Miller Williams, copyright 1958, 1961, 1962, 1965, 1966, 1967 by Nicanor Parra.

— to the McGraw-Hill Book Co. for permission to quote from Eldridge Cleaver, *Soul on Ice*, copyright 1968 by Eldridge Cleaver.

— to Keller-Crescent Co. for permission to quote from Mary Carmel Browning, *Kentucky Authors: a History of Kentucky Literature*, copyright 1968 by Sister Mary Carmel Browning.

— to the Catholic University of America Press for permission to quote from *The New Catholic Encyclopedia*, copyright 1967 by the Catholic University of America.

— to Hawthorn Books for permission to quote from George Panichas, ed., *Mansions of the Spirit*, copyright 1967 by the University of Maryland.

— to Henry Regnery Co. for permission to quote from "War and the Crisis of Language," in *The Critique of War*, ed. Robert Ginsberg, copyright 1969 by Robert Ginsberg, copyright 1969 by the trustees of the Merton Legacy Trust.

— to Harcourt, Brace, Jovanovich for permission to quote from Mark Van Doren, *Autobiography*, copyright 1939, 1944, 1948, 1953, 1957, 1958 by Mark Van Doren.

— to Farrar, Straus and Giroux for permission to quote from Robert Giroux, "Introduction," *Flannery O'Connor: The Complete Stories*, copyright 1971 by Robert Giroux.

This book has been published with the help of a grant from the Canadian Federation for the Humanities, using funds provided by the Social Sciences and Humanities Research Council of Canada.

(Photo by Ralph Eugene Meatyard)

Thomas Merton

Preface

THIS IS A GENERAL LITERARY introduction to the writings
of Thomas Merton. As opposed to a purely chronological approach, the study is designed to show Merton's versatility in
mastering various literary forms—novel, diary, essay, and poem
—as well as to reveal something of his ideas about art. Nevertheless, within the separate contexts of each of these literary modes
the works are taken up in chronological order.

The section on Merton's expository writing provided the
greatest difficulty since there is such an enormous amount of
material. I have tried to give some idea of the writers Merton was
interested in and to illuminate his principal themes and
methods. It is impossible in this sort of study to do justice to the
relationships between Merton and those writers from whom he
borrowed ideas and those writers whom he in turn influenced;
such specialized matters will doubtlessly be the basis of a
number of future books and articles on Merton. All that one can
do here is to hint at the larger connections and to make the
general outline of Merton's thought and art apparent.

My thanks go to Dr. Robert Daggy, Curator of the Merton
Room, Bellarmine College, Louisville, to Brother Patrick Hart of
the Abbey of Gethsemani, and to Merton's friends, Sister
Thérèse Lentfoehr, Bob Lax, and Ron Seitz for their help in the
preparation of this book.

Contents

For Gisela

Contemplative and Artist

THOMAS MERTON WAS BORN in Prades, France, January 31, 1915, the son of two artists, a New Zealander and an American. His mother died when he was six, and he spent his youth and adolescence as something of a nomad, living alternately with his father in various transatlantic settings and with his mother's family on Long Island. His father died in England when Thomas was 16. He was educated at private schools in France and England, at Cambridge, and at Columbia, where he obtained the M.A. degree in 1939, having written his thesis on William Blake. At Columbia he began a lifelong friendship with the distinguished literary critic Mark Van Doren. From 1939 to 1941 he taught English at St. Bonaventure University in upstate New York, and at the same time contributed reviews to the *New York Times Book Review* and other literary organs.

Outwardly he seemed headed for a successful career as a university teacher and scholar. Van Doren, for one, thought very highly of his prospects, noting in retrospect that he had "never known a mind more brilliant, more beautiful, more serious, more playful."[1] However, on December 10, 1941, Merton entered the Abbey of Gethsemani south of Louisville and immersed himself in the life of a Trappist monk until his accidental death in 1968.

Merton's vocation involved isolation from the world, silence, austerity, contemplation, and obedience to his superiors. The contemplative in him had need of a deep and lasting silence, whereas the artist felt the need to celebrate his solidarity with everyone, with those very people whom he had left behind upon entering the monastery. This ambivalence was to remain with him all of his life, and while it was a source of some anxiety to Merton himself, it is one of the strongest centers of excitement in

1

approaching his work as well as being one of the clearest ways in which to see his role in twentieth century letters.

The physical conditions of the monastic life were arduous, particularly in the 1940s before the monastery was renovated and when it produced little revenue. Merton felt more at home then at Gethsemani than in the 1950s and 1960s, when the abbey's assets appreciated significantly under the modernizing hand of Dom James Fox, who transformed the monastery from a medieval farm into a mechanized and efficient agricultural operation. The machines bothered Merton — the thought of them as much as the noise they produced.

In the 1940s life at Gethsemani was physically demanding and the diet poor, a situation that was particularly hard on Merton with his allergies to certain foods. The monks slept on straw and boards in long dormitories. The monastery was marginally heated in the bitter Kentucky winters, and there was no relief in the torrid summers when the monks worked in the fields in mid-July wearing heavy robes; they were eventually given permission to wear lighter clothes in the summer.

Because of his frail health and obvious literary ability, Merton (who was known as Father Louis to his fellow monks) was given the task of writing pious books about little known Cistercian saints and studies of the monastic life. These assignments relieved him from some of the heavy chores in the fields, but plunged him into a dilemma, since he was ordered by his superiors to continue that very work—writing—which he felt he had given up upon entering the monastic life. Therefore, he forced himself to try to keep up with his rigorous monastic routine and added the abbot's writing assignments to his already busy day, even when he was sick. In Lent the fast lasted until noon, after the monks had already spent many hours working in the fields and participating in various liturgical and contemplative activities. They rose at two in the morning. In this early period Merton completed his writing assignments in the abbey's unheated library, where some days it was so cold that he had to take the typewriter over to one of the windowsills on the east side of the building to see if the sun that came through the icy windowpane would give him a little warmth.

Eventually he was put in charge of the training of novices and scholastics, a position in the community second only to that of the abbot. As early as 1947 he wrote to Mark Van Doren that he had to confront the problem of "not becoming that middle aged professional monk whose shadow I thought I was escaping."[2] Of his over 50 books and more than 300 articles, the greater part involve expository writing even though he felt most comfortable with himself in writing poetry and keeping his journal. Nevertheless, an examination of his notebooks reveals that he moved easily and instinctively from poem to essay and from journal entry to anecdote. Generally, he felt the surge of one type of artistic activity a stimulus for other types. He told his poet friend Robert Lax that his poems helped his calligraphies, his calligraphies helped his poems, and his calligraphies helped his manifestos.[3]

In the 1940s and 1950s Merton was given two hours a day to take care of his writing assignments: "In those two hours," he wrote, "I have to take care also of correspondence, duties of charity (reading manuscripts) or obedience, proofs, contracts, photos for illustrations, talk to the printer on occasion — and I order books, and resist the temptation to read catalogues and scraps of magazines."[4] He seems to have had few people to talk to about literary matters at the monastery, even when the rule of silence was somewhat relaxed in the 1950s and 1960s. He made up for this lack in being an energetic if somewhat eclectic reader and note-taker, and by the 1960s he had developed relationships with a number of writers and artists outside the monastery, some of them close by, like the Kentucky poets Wendell Berry and Ronald Seitz. In addition in the 1960s he corresponded with a number of distinguished authors, including some, like Boris Pasternak, of international reputation.

Apart from the fact that the writing prescribed by his superiors put Merton into something of a dilemma, he was haunted by a wholly inner ambivalence. He had dearly wanted to be a writer: "There is something in my nature," he confided, "that gets the keenest and sharpest pleasure out of achievement, out of work finished and printed and distributed and read."[5] His friend and editor Naomi Burton recalled of the young Merton that he had "passionately wanted to be published and had never appeared to doubt for one minute that he was destined to be a successful author."[6] Merton was one of those people who had to write, "no matter what the obstacles."[7]

Although his superiors left him relatively free after the mid-1950s to write whatever he pleased, various journals sought contributions from him throughout his later years, and he often generously complied, frequently in the case of rather obscure publications. This sort of pressure to produce always brought about the same reaction in him—a desire for solitude—which in turn was followed by a flurry of writing activity and renewed contacts with the world around him.

Merton's writing was intimately connected with his sense of his own identity. Why did he, supposedly a man of silence, write so prolifically? He decided that it was to "make everything accessible. Why? To be recognized as a member of the human race, I guess. To have a living identity."[8] The writing was a way of staying close to those he had left behind at the gates of the monastery. In this connection he wrote in his notebook in 1968 about the "bad poetry one writes in order to *hide* love, to hide the need for love, to make oneself loved because one is a good poet not a lover."[9]

There were occasions when the monastic life seemed ideal for the sort of writing that he did. The interval between night and dawn, a very active time for monks, was especially fruitful:

> After two or three hours of prayer your mind is saturated in peace and the richness of the liturgy. The dawn is breaking outside the cold windows. If it is warm, the birds are already beginning to sing. Whole blocks of imagery seem to crystallize out as it were naturally in the silence and the peace, and the lines almost write themselves.[10]

Merton's cenobitic calling circumscribed his writing in an even more decisive and unusual way than has been indicated thus far. His order felt itself responsible for all the publications of its members and showed its interest through an elaborate system of censorship. Although the pressure of censorship eased during the 1960s, Merton bristled under it for most of his career. He announced shortly before his death that he had had "a great deal of trouble with censors within the order."[11] Judging by the bits of evidence that survived, the early censorship was oppressive. One of the censors who read *The Sign of Jonas*, for example, objected to it not on theological or moral grounds, as was his province, but on literary grounds. He noted that Merton's literary comments, particularly those on Robert Lowell, would bore most readers, and he went on to point out that many of Merton's reflections were trivial and that he was guilty of showmanship.

This overstepping by censors infuriated Merton, and he complained in a letter to Naomi Burton that the problem about order censorship was that it concentrated not on faith and morals but on a vague category called "opportunité," that is to say whether it was opportune for a particular book to be published. Anything at all, "with or without reasons given," he concluded, could cause a book to be stopped under this rubric.[12] The system of censorship was hierarchical so that even if a book was passed by the U.S. censors it could be blocked at the order's headquarters in France. It was only through the courtly intervention of Jacques Maritain to the Abbot General in France, for example, that *The Sign of Jonas* was published in the early 1950s.

The Seven Storey Mountain emerged in a bowdlerized state because of pressure brought to bear by the censors, who thought it a "very bad book" that would "do a lot of harm" even in its revised state.[13] Edward Rice, a close friend of Merton's, has said that as much as a third of *The Seven Storey Mountain* was cut out by the Trappist censors. According to Merton himself, one of the censors upon first reading the book asked that it be withheld not on theological grounds but on the basis of its being unripe for publication, with the explanation that Merton lacked the literary ability to write an effective autobiography. Another, more fundamental objection was that he had been "too frank" about his past.[14] The result, Rice concluded, was that many people wondered what kind of neurotic Merton had been to feel such guilt for reading Freud, Hemingway, D.H. Lawrence, and some Italian pornographic novels and for having a series of mild flirtations.[15]

The censorship issue came to a head in the 1960s when Merton felt compelled to question whether or not the use of nuclear weapons could be justified even in what was judged a just war. He presented his thesis in a book called "Peace in the Post-Christian Era," which was ready for publication in 1963. He was denied permission to publish it, principally because of the opposition of the Abbot General. He was bitter about it:

> I am told by a higher superior: "It is not your place to write about nuclear war: that is for the bishops."
> I am told by a moral theologian: "How can you expect the bishops to commit themselves on the question of peace and war, unless they are advised by theologians?"
> Meanwhile the theologians sit around and preserve their reputations.[16]

He felt urgently that no one in the Church was expounding his point of view on modern weaponry and that it might be too late before someone got around to doing it. A look at the unpublished manuscript of "Peace in the Post-Christian Era" reveals the sort of pronouncements that might have antagonized some of the U.S. Catholic hierarchy, whose silence Merton believed amounted to an endorsement of U.S. foreign policy in the 1950s and 1960s. "A Christian," he wrote, "ought to consider whether nuclear war is not in itself a moral evil so great that it *cannot* be justified even for the best of ends, even to defend the highest and most sacrosanct of values."[17] An underlying irony was that he drew principally upon Christian theological sources to support his thesis.

He was blocked by directives that emerged from the 1960 meeting of Trappist abbots in which it was agreed that there would be no publication by monks except where this directly concerned the order, since to do otherwise would violate the climate of silence in which the monks were expected to live. Secondly, no "rash" doctrine was to be published, nothing that would give rise to controversy. Merton was vulnerable on both counts. A look at censors' reports on his writing in the area of war and peace reveals, however, that the objection to some of the material was not simply that it would give rise to controversy but that the censors disagreed with Merton's conclusions.

While Merton was denied permission to write about nuclear warfare, he was eventually allowed to write about other issues related to war and peace and race relations. He conceded later that eventually he published nearly everything he wanted to—in some form or other. In the case of "Peace in the Post-Christian Era," for example, large chunks of it surfaced in *Seeds of Destruction* as well as in a number of articles published between 1963 and 1965. Writing for small magazines became a way of avoiding the censors. He described this in a letter to his poet friend Ernesto Cardenal in 1965, noting that he had taken to availing himself of a clause in the censorship statute of the order that ordained that short pieces published in small magazines did not have to be passed by the censors.[18]

Similarly, in 1957, when the Abbot General withheld permission for the publication of *The Secular Journal* (three out of four censors were against publishing it), Merton urged Catherine Doherty, whom he had given rights over the material, to ignore the order and do what she wanted. Fortunately she decided to publish. By the late 1960s Merton felt finally liberated from the censors and wrote to Naomi Burton in 1967 that he did not anticipate trouble in publishing his novel *My Argument with the Gestapo* "because one of the few places where there has been some liberalization for real has been in the American Censor department."[19] Nevertheless, he complained in connection with as late a work as the *Seeds of Destruction* (1965) that certain chapters were revised repeatedly in order to satisfy the censors.

Merton's acutest problems with writing were the result of his own anxieties about his dual vocation as both contemplative and author. It was not just that writing took time away from contemplation but that it seemed at a certain point to subvert it. From the beginning of his life in the monastery he had thought deeply about the relationship between art and the contemplative life, searching his experience to discover whether or not the two kinds of activity were mutually supportive. He relied heavily upon the insights of Jacques Maritain, especially those in Maritain's *Creative Intuition in Art and Poetry*, to sort out his own ideas. This reliance may not have been entirely a good idea. Maritain's orderly mind, which had been honed on medieval philosophy, was fundamentally different from Merton's, which was intuitive and tentative. Merton picked up much of Maritain's scholastic terminology and tried to make some sense out of his relationship to art as a contemplative, but he failed.

It was clear to Merton that contemplation had much to offer the germinating ideas of the artist. The question was, however: what could artistic activity do for the contemplative? Something surely, but was it enough? The artist's ingrained aesthetic taste would be a help. It would detach him from coarseness and sentimentality. Furthermore, aesthetic experience introduced one into the "interior sanctuary of the soul and to its inexpressible simplicity and economy and energy and fruitfulness."[20] In his more sanguine moments Merton affirmed that art opened up "new capacities and new areas in the person of the contemplative."[21] This effect was due to the fruitfulness of the artist's imagination, that could discover "correspondences, symbols and meanings" which in turn became "nuclei" around which the contemplative's perceptions could orbit.[22] Moreover, the artist was akin to the mystic because of the "prophetic intuition" by which he saw the spiritual reality, the inner meaning of the object that he contemplated.[23]

In mystics like William Blake and St. John of the Cross Merton saw united the fine threads of the artistic as well as the contemplative life. In such men, he believed, it is "hard to distinguish between the inspiration of the prophet and mystic, and the purely poetic enthusiasm of great artistic genius." Thus, St. John of the Cross is "the greatest poet as well as the greatest contemplative."[24]

There were occasions when Merton felt dejectedly that it was not easy to live the spiritual life with the equipment of an artist. His journals, especially in earlier years, are filled with references to abandoned poems, accompanied by vows to shut down this sort of creative activity, followed in turn by a change of mind and a new round of creative productivity, The problem was one of guilt. Was he not betraying his vocation in devoting his energies to such things as the writing of poetry? If it was true that aesthetic perception could purify mystical contemplation, it could also cut it short by tempting the artist to use his fresh perceptions for the making of a work of art instead of sacrificing his insights for the further ascent of mystical heights and the attainment of his union with God. The artist ran the risk of losing "a gift of tremendous supernatural worth in order to perform a work of far less value."[25] Intent upon turning his contemplative experience into a poem or a painting, the artist objectified that experience and sought to "exploit and employ it for its own sake." In following his instinct to create, the artist abbreviated the creative work done in the soul and on the soul by God. The result was a premature return by the contemplative to a world of "multiple created things" whose variety once more dissipated his energies until they were lost in "perplexity and dissatisfaction."[26]

In his stirring first discussion of his dilemma, an essay called "Poetry and the Contemplative Life" (1947), Merton felt that there was no way out. His only recourse, he believed, was the sacrifice of his art. It is widely believed that his later essay "Poetry and Contemplation: A Reappraisal" (1958) articulated a solution to his rather subtle metaphysical problem. In point of fact, the problem remained intellectually insoluble for him until his death. The solution came in his behavior and in the value he ascribed to his dilemma. It began to emerge earlier than 1958, when he wrote his revised statement on poetry and contempla-tion. He had written Mark Van Doren in the summer of 1948 that, although he still held to everything he had said in "Poetry and the Contemplative Life" about the nature of the problem, he was "beginning to see everything in a strangely different light. I can no longer see the ultimate meaning of a man's life in terms of either 'being a poet' or 'being a contemplative.'" Instead, he concluded, each man must be allowed to have his "own, special, peculiar destiny."[27]

Merton overcame his difficulty by moving away from the looming philosophical abstractions that had confounded him — to his own ground, so to speak, his instinct for experience rather than for metaphysical speculation. Neither religious nor artistic contemplation should be regarded as "things" that happen or as "objects" that one can possess. Instead, these belong to the mysterious realm of "what one 'is' — or rather 'who' one is."[28] He wrote to an inquirer in 1964 that the configuration of his life demanded a "synthesis of poetry and prayer," even if this meant, as it surely did for him, a rejection of a "technically" higher kind of life if he continued as an artist.[29] The synthesis of his talents and energies would be justified in and by the life that he led rather than on a level of subtle abstract formulation.

The nature of art and the relationship of the artist to society were a continuing interest of Merton's from the time of his M.A. thesis on William Blake, which turned out to be an informal and stimulating discussion of aesthetics. Antecedent to his curiosity about the nature of art was his consciousness of the artist's role in his society, a subject that he never tired of taking up. The reason was that he felt a profound intimacy between the roles of religion and art in relation to the vitality of the whole society. His notebooks reveal that he had a profound distaste for aesthetic norms that existed in a moral void. He came to feel that in a technocracy such as that evolved by twentieth century man some form of religious idealism was necessary to sustain art. He sympathized with contemporary artists who fled from the sterility and vulgarity of their civilization, but he felt that, in the absence of any alternative value systems, these artists were destined to vanish in the dead world of subjective abstraction.

In addition, in some unpublished notes on art Merton deplored the fragmentation of modern life, the "utter lack of relatedness between various phases of life and thought" and the existence of "hundreds of insignificant philosophies, each with a different set of terms." In the face of this fragmentation Merton believed that the artist reacted as he always did — "like a seismograph."[30]

The artist registered the collapse of meaning in his culture without being able to do much about it, and his sensitivity went largely unnoticed in any case. Merton lamented the way in which, all too often, original talents went off on their own, experimenting as they pleased, with results which were often very fruitful aesthetically, but which had "little or no effect on the life or thought of the majority of men."[31]

Merton felt that there was something vaguely pathological about modern man's obsession with creativity in an age devoted to unprecedented destructiveness, but he believed that even this condition was a sign of man's unquenchable interest in art. He saw the need for art as basic to man and argued that, if man could not have good art; he would "jealously defend the bad."[32] He admired the traditional Japanese concept of art in which there

was no divorce between art and life, nor between art and spirituality, and he preferred this to the academic and solipsistic direction which he felt much western art had taken. Similarly, he felt
closer to Latin American poets than to those in North America
because in Latin America the voice of the poet had "something to do with life," whereas the North American artist appeared to be in a "spiritual torpor."[33]

Merton believed that art did things for society that could not be
done in any other way. The work of art helped to elevate and
clarify the intelligence and heart both of the artist and of the
spectator. In this way the art experience became "analogous to
the purity of religious contemplation."[34] He focused his attention on the experiential value of the poem or the painting: "A
poem is for me," he once wrote, "the expression of an inner
poetic experience, and what matters is the experience, more than
the poem itself."[35]

He saw the life of the artist as a sharing of himself with others.
He expressed this vividly in a poem entitled "The Originators:"

> Brothers and Sisters I warn you my ideas
> Get scarlet fever every morning
> At about four and influence goes out of my windows
> Over the suburbs . . .
> And when the other's nerve ends crowed and protested
> In the tame furies of a business gospel
> His felling was my explosion.[36]

The impact of artist on reader is symbiotically paralleled by that
of the reader on the artist so that the "explosion" of the artist
inside the spectator is followed by a boomerang effect in which:
"I skidded off his stone head/Blind as a bullet/But found I was
wearing his hat."

The reader of course had to make an effort to be intelligently
receptive. The artist, Merton felt, had no obligation to make his
meaning immediately clear to anyone who did not want to make
an effort to discover it. On the other hand the esoteric artist who
cultivated obscurity deprived not only others but himself: "If
you know something and do not share it," he wrote, "you lose

11

your knowledge of it."[37]

Although Merton believed in the prophetic role of the artist, he stood firmly against didacticism: "The artist should preach nothing—not even his own autonomy."[38] The contamination of art by dogma of any sort was, he felt, a matter about which the artist had to be ever vigilant. "When a Marxist-poet writes as a Marxist," he wrote to a friend, "he ceases to write as a poet," and that "goes for every other brand of dogmatism that imposes itself on art *from without*."[39] The most significant Catholic writers, he believed, were people who wrote as "marginal or unusual Catholics, and do not speak for the mass of our brethren."[40] The artist could not succeed by "wearing the garments of public and collective ideas"[41] and should do everything in his power to resist the pull of these ideas, creating his work always "outside and against the officially subsidized culture."[42]

Merton saw the prophetic role of the artist as a natural one for the contemporary artist to assume amidst the decline in the authority of religion. At the same time there were dangers in a "myth of the genius as hero and as high priest" that took the place of religion.[43] Certain modern writers, like Faulkner and Camus, were singled out by Merton as genuinely prophetic. He wrote to the poet Nicanor Parra in 1965 that contemporary artists tended to fulfill many of the functions that were once the monopoly of monks.[44] He went further: "I would submit that the term 'religious' no longer conveys the idea of an imaginative awareness of basic meaning. As D. H. Lawrence asserted, 'It's not religious to be religious.'"[45] As religion had attempted to do, the artist perceived man in terms of the wholeness of his life, a kind of vision which was uniquely valuable in a culture dominated by specialists.

A writer like Faulkner, therefore, could be profoundly biblical in his work without being a churchgoer or a conventional believer. It was the artist, "facing the problems of life without the routine consolations of conventional religion," who experienced in depth the "existential dimensions of those problems."[46] This outlook led Merton to shift his attention from formally religious texts to literary models. He wrote to James Laughlin in 1966 that he and Jacques Maritain, who had just visited with him, both agreed that perhaps the most "living" way to approach theological and philosophical problems now that theology and philosophy were in such chaos would be in the form of "creative writing and literary criticism."[47]

It was axiomatic for Merton that the artist had to be a spiritual man. In addition, writers like Faulkner and Camus were prophetic in the sense that in constructing myths in which they embodied their struggle with the fundamental questions of life they anticipated "in their solitude" the struggles and the general consciousness of later generations.[48] The artist had inherited, whether he liked it or not, the combined functions of hermit, pilgrim, prophet, priest, shaman, sorcerer, soothsayer, alchemist, and bonze.[49] The temptation for the artist who was aware of these roles to give in to posturing was obvious to Merton, and the moral solution was for the artist to concentrate on his proper "work" rather than on the role which society asked him to play.

Merton felt that the purity of the artist's vision could only be sustained through a kind of "ingrained innocence," by which he meant a freshness and seriousness of vision in the artist that could withstand the banalities of his society.[50] Given these circumstances, the artist would prophesy, not in the sense of preaching or foretelling, but in seizing upon reality "in its moment of highest expectation and tension toward the new."[51]

The artist as prophet would show finally "where everything connects," a reflection of Merton's own passionate role as a unifier of different kinds of experience.[52] The artist could do all of this because in his "innocence" he perceived the paradise that had been and that was still present beneath the welter of sordid and fragmentary details that made up modern life. Merton saw the artist's creation as both analogous to the freshness of paradise and a sign of its possible recovery:

> [The] living line and the generative association, the new sound, the music, the structure, are somehow grounded, in a renewal of vision and hearing so that he who reads and understands recognizes that here is a new start, a new creation. Here the world gets another chance. Here man, here the reader discovers himself getting another start in life, in hope, in imagination.[53]

13

Merton spoke of the poet as attempting to dream the world in which he lived. That dream, though intensely personal, was at once the artist's and everybody's, a paradise accessible to all, once the poet had recovered it. The freshness and power of the artist's vision in recovering the fragrance of a lost and perfect world came home to Merton in 1960 when he collaborated with the photographer Shirley Burden in a pictorial study of the Abbey of Gethsemani. When the book came out, Merton was struck with the difference between his own faded perceptions of the abbey and those which Burden manifested:

And now a man, an artist, comes along with a camera and shows us, beyond a doubt, that the real monastery, the one that is so obvious that we no longer see it, the one that has become so familiar that we have not even looked at it for years, is not only beautiful, but romantically beautiful. It is romantic even in the ordinariness, the banality that we ourselves tend to reject.[54]

Merton saw the artist as evoking a sense of the latent perfection of things. The business of the artist was "to reach the intimate," that is, those "ontological sources of life" that could not be clearly conceptualized, but which, once intuited, could be made "accessible to all in symbolic celebration."[55] Good art expressed the singular. The singularity of the experience suspended within the poem or picture was paralleled by the inner principle of individuality in the form of the poem or picture. Through structure and symbol the artist wrested language from its faded and worn contexts in order to make it new. Language had to be freed from contamination by trite popular discourse and yet had also to serve its prior purpose of sharing experience with the reader.

The artist, Merton believed, went out to the object before him — a rose or a grain of sand — with complete humility, not subjecting the object to the classifying habit of the mind, but so identifying with it as to look out of it as though the artist fulfilled the role of consciousness not only for himself but for the object as well. In this way the artist became "the conscious expression, not of himself seeing and singing, but of the singing being which is his object and inspiration. He feels *'for,'* sings *'for,'* is aware *'for'* the object."[56] This identification of natures emerged from experience rather than meditation in the same way that "a chaste man understands the nature of chastity because of the very fact that his soul is full of it."[57] The process involved a marvellous accommodation between the artist and the world around him as well as a momentary union of the contraries within the artist — akin, Merton wrote in his notebook, to the kind of ecstacy experienced by "mystics, children, lovers."[58]

While genuine art illuminated reality, Merton felt that little of this effect could be traced back to the artist's conscious intentions. At least 75 per cent of the process of creation, he told a group of students in the mid-1960s, was unconscious. If this were reduced to only 30 per cent, he told the class, the art would be bad.[59] He wrote in his notebook in the same period that the creation of a work of art went far beyond the artist's understanding: "Hence to be an artist you have to be constantly ready to *mean more than you realize.* If your work corresponds only to the present level of your thought—and to the 'meaning' accessible to your environment, you are not yet an artist."[60] In the spectator as well genuine art reached beneath the conscious mind to the darkness of the psyche in order to do its unique and necessary work.

Merton loved the mysterious way in which art drew things together. In a diary written in the last year of his life he described his pleasure in seeing a print of a photo he had taken of the northern California coast that had been developed for him by his friend John Howard Griffin. The film brought out the "sea-rock mist, diffused light and half hidden mountain . . . an interior landscape, yet there." "In other words," he wrote, "what is written within me is there."[61] It was probably because of Merton's respect for the mystery of the artistic process that he came to place such emphasis upon spontaneity in art. His calligraphies represent the epitome of the spontaneous in his work, and his prolific output in general suggests great speed in the act of creation throughout his career — not always to the benefit of the works produced. He hoped to tap the riches of the subconscious before the conscious mind could meditate or usurp expression, and he saw this process as the secret of the Zen artist who created "without reflection." The Zen drawing, he wrote, "springs" out of emptiness, and is transferred "in a flash," by a few brush strokes, to paper. So produced, it is not a representation of anything, but is rather the subject itself, a "concretized intuition."[62]

Merton realized that such art skirted the solipsistic, and gave only a small part of his creative time to the production of such radically spontaneous works. Even in his more representational work, however, his fondness for speed and spontaneity in creation is revealed. The emergence of a work of art from his hand always had in it something of an element of surprise for him: "We who are poets," he wrote on one occasion, "know that the reason for a poem is not discovered until the poem itself exists."[63] For this reason, perhaps, he shied away from protracted discussions about how he put poems together.

The subjects that the contemporary artist should take up were a matter of continuing interest to Merton. His own eclecticism makes it difficult at times to think of him as pursuing any particular line, but he had established some guidelines for himself. He felt a need, for example, to purify religious verse from what he felt had become an "insatiable emotional vulgarity."[64] Twentieth century religious verse, he believed, had for too long been singing the "same old cracked tune that the Georgians inherited from Tennyson and Swinburne."[65] At the same time he disdained the "flood tide of spurious and pseudomodern sacred art" that had begun to show itself in religious literature, music, painting, and architecture.[66] Churches that were constructed to resemble other undistinguished contemporary architecture — "the drive-in theater, the filling station, the motel or even the night club" — were hardly an improvement over the earlier absurdities of the pseudogothic and pseudoromanesque.[67]

What was needed, he wrote in an unpublished manuscript entitled "The Monk and Sacred Art," was a clearing of the "confusion" surrounding religious art so that "what belongs to us and what is alien to us" can be discerned in the art of the past as well as of the present.[68] The first requirement was for the artist to attend to his craft instead of hoping that his piety would alchemically produce fine works of art. In this respect he was drawn to the Hindu tradition of art in which all artistic work became a form of yoga. In such a tradition, he observed, "there ceases to be any distinction between sacred and secular art. All art is Yoga, and even the art of making a table or a bed, or building a house, proceeds from the craftsman's Yoga and from his spiritual discipline of meditation."[69] Religious art should emerge, he felt, only from the crucible of experience. If not, he argued in *Bread in the Wilderness*, it was third-rate, merely devotional art which, although it dealt with religious themes, was often simply the "rearrangement of well known devotional formulas, without any personal poetic assimilation."[70]

As an artist Merton applied himself to trying to restore the face of nature and the rhythm of natural time as against the abrasive and synthetic pattern of modern life. Art should, he felt, ideally be grounded in the natural world and should represent the flowering of ordinary possibilities. Opposing himself to the artificiality of technocracy, he called on artists to refrain from trying to "make the tree bear its fruit first and the flower afterwards. "We are content as artists," he wrote, "if the flower comes first and the fruit afterwards, in due time. Such is the poetic spirit."[71]

It was this instinct to conserve which attracted him to Classicism, the signs of which are everywhere in his writings. Merton came to see Classicism as the mainstream in which the values of Western civilization were kept alive, and he was grateful for this continuity in a culture in which collapse and dislocation seemed the rule. He was especially impressed by T. S. Eliot's ability to combine a sense of the past with a highly modern, experimental attitude toward form, a combination which he tried to achieve in his own writing. He liked the Classicism as well of more recent poets like Edward Dahlberg, whose work was "juiced with myth and with the lore of the fathers who know better than we."[72]

There were Romantic elements in Merton's thought, notably in his penchant for spontaneity. The problem with Classicism was that it possessed a deliberate, static quality that seemed unexciting to him. In addition, his notebooks reveal that he was attracted to the impressionistic strain in Romanticism, its ability to "marry subject and object through the image" — as long, that is, as this marriage did not end in the closed circuit of the subjec-

17

tive.[73] With his instinct for balance and unity, he gradually adjusted his outlook in order to accommodate both Classic and Romantic elements.

Seen from another vantage point, Merton affirmed the existence of a Classicism which was more dynamic than that which has been conventionally described. In a little known, privately printed note on the artist Victor Hammer he depicted Classicism not as a serene pool of light and reason but as an arena in which matter and energy with their own compelling truths were not dispelled by the light of consciousness. Thus, from the body of the "python," the "earth dragon," there would emanate a "living voice of prophecy." This prophetic voice was eloquent and significant in proportion to the force of the "darkness" which drew upon itself the "discipline of the strongest light."[74]

Merton believed that the art object should be "organic" — that is, that it should develop the way a living organism does so that it spread outward in a "heliotropic" manner like a plant. "A tree," he wrote, "grows out into a free form, an organic form," one that is "never ideal," "never typical," and "always individual."[75] He disliked purely naturalistic art. To copy nature, he believed, was to falsify it. The artist should not reproduce, but he should create something new. Paradoxically, the realism of the artist's creation depended upon its ability to suggest rather than to copy, since what was real in such a case was not simply the art object but the "experience of the one looking at it."[76]

In Merton's view nothing resembled reality less than the photograph. In his own photographs — studies of roots, tree limbs, and faded barns — he concentrated on the texture of these simple things with such imagination and freedom that they resemble abstract paintings. This effect can be seen in the tree ring photograph that he provided for the dustjacket of Nicanor Parra's *Poems and Antipoems.*

Merton felt that the way out of the cul-de-sac of naturalism was through symbol, a fact which he believed even the most primitive peoples seemed to understand better than contemporary Western man. He tried to explain the transcendental effect of symbolism in describing the role of the ikon in Russian Orthodox churches. He described the ikon as more than a representation, conveying the "spiritual presence" of the figure represented, a presence that has mysteriously clothed itself in the lines and colors used by the artist.[77] He was convinced that the search for adequate symbols should not be esoteric, contending that all things are symbolic "by their very being and nature, and all talk of something beyond themselves." Their meaning, he added, is not something we impose on them, but a "mystery which we can discover in them, if we have the eyes to look with."[78]

He perceived the artist's challenge as avoiding those symbols which had been debased by society and the marketplace. He wrote to a friend that he was "right to go at it with myth and symbol" since this sort of writing was the only thing conventional society could not "monkey with" even though it tried.[79] A similar furtiveness underlay Merton's experiments in calligraphy, which he characterized as original and "nondescript" marks that stood against the mass of "practical signs and consequential digits" that were used in business, law, government, and war. His drawings were at least "new" signs, signs that could stand by themselves and exist in their own right, "transcending" all logical interpretation.[80]

If it became evident to the artist that his society had contaminated most of the available language, he would have to resort to anti-language, as Merton chose to do in *Cables to the Ace* (1968), a poetic sequence written in what he called "antipoetry." Pushed to the wall, the artist might have no choice but to use "anti-art and non-symbol."[81] Merton believed that twentieth century man had lost touch with the fertile mainstream of Western symbolism. By way of exception he admired T. S. Eliot's ability, especially in the *Four Quartets*, to use traditional symbols to rise above the limitations of contemporary experience in order to achieve a "deliverance from a commonplace and fictitious identity in the stream of historical continuity."[82]

Merton saw the modern artist as frustrated in his search for the vital symbols that he believed had been buried alive amid the contemporary hunger for information and explanation. He pictured the most gifted artists of the age as driven by desperation, "running wild among the tombs in the moonlit cemeteries of surrealism."[83] The flight from conventional symbolism became perverse and self-defeating, however, since the artist and his audience both had a basic human need for myth and symbol. In becoming instinctively suspicious of that "for which we are starved," the artist may simply aggravate his problem in communicating.[84] Lamenting that ancient symbols had lost their meaning, the artist may become "hostile and uncommunicative, frustrating the desire for meaning by declaring that there are no meanings left and that one has to get along without them."[85]

The corruption of cosmic symbolism led to the loss of transcendental perception. Merton illustrated this conception in terms of the passing of light through a window: "As long as it is daylight, we see through our windowpane. When night comes, we can still see through it, if there is no light inside our room. When our lights go on, then we only see ourselves and our own room reflected in the pane."[86] The corruption of cosmic symbolism could not be blamed simply on secularism, but pointed unavoidably to a loss of vitality within the social institutions that thrived on it at one time, including Christianity.

This loss seemed both unnecessary and harmful to Merton. He revealed this conviction in a poem called "The Lion," which he wrote in 1967:

> All classic shapes have vanished
> From alien heavens
> When there are no fabled beasts
> No friendly histories
> And passion has no heraldry.[87]

Poised to write, he finds that he has "nothing left to translate/ Into the figures of the night" since the traditional astronomical symbolism that had been at the heart of Western literature is no longer recognized by contemporary men. Looking up at the sky, he sees the constellation of Taurus and wonders why the image of the Lion in the night sky should ever have been put aside, observing that Gemini as well was astutely named by the ancients: "It is after all a Lion/ And those two stars are permanent;/ Let us agree they are twins." It was not just that these symbols had come down from the early Babylonians and that the use of them brought men of the past and present together in spirit, but that the symbols were still fresh in that they could be experienced anew by modern stargazers.

It was only through effective symbolism, Merton believed, that the deepest riches of man's unconscious life could be reached, and it was only within the dark world that there was hope of recovering an awareness of man's fundamental nature and needs. As basic archetypal forms anterior to any operation of the mind, the symbols used by the artist awakened buried feelings within the reader's unconscious and revived his strongest memories of himself as a creature. In caressing the reader's unconscious, the artist awakened the reader to the form-less world of being by suggesting through symbol what could not be said. "We are children of the Unspeakable," Merton wrote, "ministers of silence."[88]

Merton saw this underlying feeling of being, the meeting place of all life, as evoked not only through effective symbolism but through a complex interaction of speech and silence, object and emptiness. Silence, he observed paradoxically, was the "mother of speech."[89] Life, he wrote, is not to be regarded as an uninter-rupted flow of words which is finally silenced by death. Instead, its rhythm "develops in silence, comes to the surface in moments of necessary expression" and then returns to "deeper silence."[90] He did not intend to undervalue the force of language, but rather to establish a balance between language and silence. If it was true that the reality that was inexpressible in language was found "face to face and without medium" in silence, it was also true that this reality would not ordinarily be discovered "in itself, that is to say in its own silence," unless one were first brought to it through language.[91] In one of his taped lectures he took the view that a good poem was 50 per cent silence and that what was not said in a literary work was just as important as what was made explicit, if not more important. The silence on the page had to be attuned to the rhythms of silence and expressiveness that were rooted in experience. In introducing the Japanese edition of *Thoughts in Solitude*, he noted that the book said nothing that had not already been said better "by the wind in the pine trees. Its pages seek nothing more than to echo the silence and the peace that is 'heard' when rain wanders freely among the hills and forests."[92]

When set within its natural context of silence, Merton felt that

21

all language was "intrinsically poetic."[93] At the same time, in order to offset the jadedness of conventional expression, language had to be lifted out of its conventional context and then restored to communicative power by its fresh use in a work of art. It was this sensitivity to silence—to what lay behind the word—that motivated Merton's art as well as his life as a contemplative. While differing in some other respects, the artist and the contemplative in him were in agreement on this matter.

Notes

[1]Mark Van Doren, "Thomas Merton," *America*, CXX (Jan. 4, 1969), p. 22.

[2]Letter to Mark Van Doren, Nov. 5, 1947.

[3]"A Catch of Anti-Letters," *Voyages*, XI (1968), p. 52.

[4]*The Sign of Jonas* (New York, 1953), p. 161.

[5]"Todo y Nada: Writing and Contemplation," *Renascence*, II (1950), p. 91.

[6]"A Note on the Author and This book," in *My Argument with the Gestapo* by Thomas Merton, (New York, 1969), p. 10.

[7]Naomi Burton-Stone, *More Than Sentinels*, (New York, 1964), p. 240.

[8]Notebook #88. Entry for January 6, 1968.

[9]Notebook #87. The entry was made in March, 1968.

[10]*The Seven Storey Mountain*, (New York, 1948), pp. 389-390.

[11]"A Conference on Prayer, Calcutta, October 27, 1968," *Sisters Today*, XLI (1970), p. 68.

[12]Letter to Naomi Burton-Stone, Jan. 7, 1964.

[13]"A Conference on Prayer," pp. 445-456.

[14]*Sign of Jonas*, p. 40.

[15]Edward Rice, *The Man in the Sycamore Tree: The Good Times and Hard Life of Thomas Merton*, (New York, 1970), p. 65.

[16]*Conjectures of a Guilty Bystander*, (New York, 1966), p. 271.

[17]"Peace in the Post-Christian Era," p. 2. Manuscript.

[18]Letter to Ernesto Cardenal, May 10, 1965.

[19]Letter to Naomi Burton-Stone, Oct. 4, 1967.

[20]"Poetry and the Contemplative Life," *Commonweal*, XLVI (July 4, 1947), p. 283.

[21]*Seeds of Contemplation* (Norfolk, Conn., 1949), pp. 342-343.

[22]Ibid., p. 346.

[23]"Poetry and Contemplation: A Reappraisal," *Commonweal*, LXIX (Oct. 24, 1958), p. 89.

[24]Ibid., p. 88.

[25]"Poetry and Contemplation: A Reappraisal," p. 91.

[26]Ibid., p. 91.

[27]Letter to Mark Van Doren, March 30, 1948.

[28]"Poetry and Contemplation: A Reappraisal," p. 87.

[29]Letter to Sister Cecilia, Jan. 31, 1964.

[30]"Notes on Sacred Art," Conferences given to Scholastics, October and November, 1954, p. 3. Mimeographed.

[31]Ibid., p. 3.

[32]Ibid., p. 3.

[33]Letter to Margaret Randall de Mondragon, Jan. 15, 1963.

[34]"Art and Morality," *New Catholic Encyclopedia*, I (1967), p. 865.

[35]Mary Carmel Browning, "Father Thomas Louis Merton: The Trappist Poet of Contemplation," in *Kentucky Authors: A History of Kentucky Literature* (Evansville, Indiana, 1968), p. 215.

[36]"The Originators," *Unicorn Folio*, Series one, No. 3 (Santa Barbara, 1967). Reprinted in *The Collected Poems of Thomas Merton* (New York, 1977), p. 613.

[37]"Letter to Friends" (Midsummer, 1967). Mimeographed.

[38]"Answers on Art and Freedom," in *Raids on the Unspeakable* (New York, 1966), p. 171.

[39]Letter to Margaret Randall de Mondragon, Oct. 9, 1963.

[40]Letter to Sister Thérèse Lentfoehr, May 12, 1967.

[41]"Message to Poets," in *Raids on the Unspeakable*, p. 161.

[42]*Conjectures of a Guilty Bystander*, p. 259.

[43]"The Catholic and Creativity: Theology of Creativity," *American Benedictine Review*, XI (1960) p. 202.

[44]Letter to Nicanor Parra, March 20, 1965.

[45]"Baptism in the Forest: Wisdom and Initiation in William Faulkner," in *Mansions of the Spirit*, ed. George Panichas (New York, 1967), p. 25.

[46]*Opening the Bible* (Collegeville, Minnesota, 1970), p. 42.

[47]Letter to James Laughlin, Oct. 8, 1966.

[48]"Can We Survive Nihilism?" *Saturday Review*, I (April 15, 1967), p. 16.

[49]"Answers on Art and Freedom," p. 173.

[50]"Message to Poets," p. 156.

[51]Ibid., p. 159.

[52]David Steindal-Rast, "Recollections of Thomas Merton's Last Days in the West," *Monastic Studies*, VII (1969), p. 2.

[53]"Paradise Bugged," *Critic*, XXV (1967), p. 69.

[54]"Introduction," *God is My Life: The Story of Our Lady of Gethsemani* by Shirley Burden (New York, 1960), unpaginated.

[55]"The True Legendary Sound: The Poetry and Criticism of Edwin Muir," *Sewanee Review*, LXXV (1967), p. 318.

23

[56]*Mystics and Zen Masters* (New York, 1967), p. 246.
[57]*Seven Storey Mountain*, p. 202.
[58]Notebook #63 (1956).
[59]Tape 194-A (Dec. 12, 1964). Lecture on Donne and poetry in general.
[60]Notebook #55 (Nov. 25, 1967).
[61]"Woods, Shore, Desert" (May, 1968), the unpublished log of Merton's first visit to California.
[62]"Catholic and Creativity," p. 206.
[63]"Message to Poets," p. 155.
[64]"Poetry and the Contemplative Life," p. 283.
[65]Ibid., p. 281.
[66]"Notes on Art and Worship," p. 8.
[67]Ibid., p. 8.
[68]"The Monk and Sacred Art," p. 231.
[69]"Notes on Art and Worship," pp. 10-11.
[70]*Bread in the Wilderness*, p. 55.
[71]"Message to Poets," pp. 159-160.
[72]"Ceremony for Edward Dahlberg," *Tri-Quarterly*, no. 19 (Fall, 1970), p. 138.
[73]Notebook #83 (1967).
[74]"Forward," *Victor Hammer: A Retrospective Exhibition* (Raleigh, North Carolina, 1965), p. 4.
[75]*The Secular Journal of Thomas Merton* (New York, 1959), p. 24.
[76]"Notes on Art and Worship," pp. 3-4.
[77]Ibid., p. 12.
[78]Letter to Mark Van Doren in 1954, quoted in Van Doren's introduction to *The Selected Poems of Thomas Merton*, (New York, 1959), p. xiii.
[79]Letter to William B. Miller, Feb. 27, 1965.
[80]"Signatures: Notes on the Author's Drawings," in *Raids on the Unspeakable*, pp. 181-182.
[81]"Symbolism: Communication or Communion?" *Monastic Exchange, II* (1970), p. 2.
[82]"Art and Worship," p. 116.
[83]*Bread in the Wilderness*, p. 59.
[84]Ibid., p. 30.
[85]*Conjectures of a Guilty Bystander*, p. 275.
[86]*Bread in the Wilderness*, p. 61.
[87]"The Lion," *Sewanee Review*, LXXV (1967), 387-388. Reprinted in the *Collected Poems*, p. 643.
[88]"Message to Poets," p.161.
[89]*No Man is an Island* (New York, 1955), p. 258.
[90]Ibid., p. 261.

[91]*Thoughts in Solitude* (New York, 1958), p. 114.
[92]Preface to the Japanese edition of *Thoughts in Solitude* (Kyoto, 1966), p. 1. Manuscript. Merton's foreign prefaces have been compiled by Robert Daggy and will be published by Unicorn Press.
[93]Notebook #83 (1967).

Narrative Writer

THOMAS MERTON'S NARRATIVE writing, which is composed chiefly of *My Argument with the Gestapo* and *The Seven Storey Mountain*, is limited to his early period. He attempted to publish three autobiographical novels in 1940 and 1941. These novels had been composed at high speed at a cottage in Olean, New York, which was owned by his friend Robert Lax's sister and brother-in-law. The first novel, *The Straits of Dover*, was sent to Harcourt, Brace, and Company, where his friend Robert Giroux was an editor. Giroux has described the work in retrospect as an autobiographical novel about a young man floundering about in New York trying to decide what to do with his life. There were scenes at Cambridge and Columbia, Merton's old haunts, and the characters included "a stupid millionaire, his wife, a showgirl, and a leftist intellectual."[1] The novel had been rejected by a first reader, and Giroux found himself unable to argue with that assessment.

At the end of 1940 Merton submitted a second novel, *The Labyrinth*, to Harcourt, Brace, and Company. It was well-named, recalls Giroux, "a dead-end version of the earlier book, whose story was unresolved and unfinished."[2] Naomi Burton, Merton's literary agent, recalls that *The Labyrinth* was an obvious commercial risk but that "all the younger editors loved it":

> It was, in parts, hilariously funny and I found that as I met more and more editors they'd say, "Oh, you're the agent who sent me that wonderful book, *The Labyrinth*." We'd talk about a scene where a character got caught in the doors leading into the Weylin Bar and shot out into the street, which was something that always seemed perfectly likely to happen on a crowded night. The outer door opened in and the inner door opened out and the hatcheck girl operated her thriving business in four square feet between the two.[3]

In April 1941 Merton's third novel, *The Man in the Sycamore Tree*, crossed Giroux's desk, but it too "did not add up to a publishable novel."[4] After a number of rejections Merton destroyed the manuscripts of these three novels just before entering Gethsemani.

In November 1941 a fourth novel, *The Journal of My Escape from the Nazis* (published in 1969 as *My Argument with the Gestapo*), came across Giroux's desk. Giroux thought it the "best of the four," but now felt convinced that "Merton was not a novelist."[5] The book was a poetic fantasy involving an imaginary visit by "Thomas Merton," a troubled young intellectual, to England and France during the Second World War. In spite of the fact that it was judged a better novel than the earlier three, the problems with publishing it in 1941 were enormous. "How could one interest anyone in a book about an *imaginary* visit to England and France," recalls Naomi Burton, when there were so many "firsthand" accounts of the war in circulation:

> To complicate matters, Tom's attitude toward the picture of brave little England and his sharp remarks on such sacred subjects as allied propaganda were considered at best puzzling, at worst downright suspicious. There was the difficulty of the macaronic passages with their jumble of English, French, Spanish, German, Italian, and who knows what else. And the double-talk — surely a sign of the impact of *Finnegans Wake* on our whole generation — did not tend to help things at all.[6]

Merton returned periodically to the thought of publishing the novel. In a letter to Mark Van Doren in 1946 he disclosed that he tried it out on a Chicago publisher who "liked it a lot and wanted me to rewrite it. But I can't rewrite a thing like that here" (in the monastery), he went on, "where would I get the proper sort of ideas?"[7] In 1959 he considered publishing it again after carrying out certain revisions. Finally, in 1967 he set about revising it, and it was scheduled for publication by Doubleday before he left for the Orient in 1968. He had heard, though, that the editors at Doubleday were unenthusiastic about publishing it.[8]

There were problems with the manuscript, because, as Merton explained in a letter written in 1968, the woman who typed the manuscript for him got the chapters in the wrong order, an unnerving occurrence in connection with a novel whose chapter order might be construed as all too arbitrary anyway.[9] Nevertheless, he straightened things out and wrote to Mark Van Doren that he thought it needed little revision, that it held up "pretty well" and that it was adapted to the world's "current frenzies"[10] — alluding to the Viet Nam war and to the climate of fear and hostility surrounding the building up of nuclear arsenals.

My Argument with the Gestapo was written in the summer of 1941, when Merton was teaching English at St. Bonaventure University in Olean, New York, and thinking about becoming a Trappist monk. He characterized the novel in retrospect as a kind of "sardonic meditation on the world in which I then found myself; an attempt to define its predicament and my own place in it."[11] The emphasis, once again, was autobiographical. Writing the book satisfied a "psychological necessity" that arose from his sense of "identification, by guilt, with what was going on in England."[12] He saw his own wild years in England as having contributed to the general decay which made war both an inevitable and just aftermath. In addition, he later wrote in his notebook that he had felt his personal connection with the two great wars to be a close one, having been born during the first and having emerged into manhood during the second. It was a time in Western civilization, he felt, when the "whole thing came to a head" and civilization trembled because of a "massive attack from within itself."[13]

At the same time, it was clear that the novel, written early in the war, was lighter in tone than events would warrant; the full horrors were yet to come. In this sense Merton felt that the book obviously could not be considered an adequate statement about Nazism and the war. What remained "actual" about the novel was its illumination of the fact that there was no "evading the universal human crisis" of which the Nazis were but "one partial symptom" (p.6). The Germany that Merton dealt with, like the England he portrayed, was largely that of the 1930s, the period of his own residence in Europe. It was the Germany that accepted Nazism.

My Argument with the Gestapo concerns a young man who returns to London during the early days of World War II and who falls under suspicion both in England and in France because of his fictitious passport and his reluctance to claim citizenship in any actual country. His diary is suspected of being subversive and becomes the focus of some alternately menacing and comic interrogations by English and French police forces as well as by the Gestapo.

The novel is a picaresque fantasy involving a narrator with a penchant for surrealistic imaginings who meanders through society illuminating not only himself but the absurd and sinister reality of those whom he encounters. As is common with this type of picaresque novel, whatever unity there is, is provided by the central character and by the themes. In addition, Merton provides underlying motifs, generating atmospheric patterns that tie the novel together effectively, more than has been recognized by the novel's commentators.

A problem with the novel is its static and unresolved quality, a problem that no one appears to have been more aware of than Merton himself. He conceded that the book lacked action. A "situation presents itself," he wrote, and the "stream of the book — which after all has a stream — stops and forms a lake."[14] There is surface movement throughout — from London to Folkestone to Paris, from the periphery of the war to its vortex, and from the present to the past — but the characters and the underlying situation remain essentially the same, whatever the superficial changes in nationality and locale. The thematic effect is to underscore the moral similarity among the participants in the war, but the narrative effect is to create monotony. The complexity of the design, though, with its interweaving of not only past and present but of the real and the unreal, the dreamed and the experienced, provides liveliness and suspense.

Structurally the novel would have been improved by lopping off Chapter 25, which is light-headed and anticlimactic, thereby concluding with Chapter 24, which focuses on the war-inflicted schizophrenia of a French soldier, clearly one of the strongest episodes in the novel. It is a remarkable chapter for a noncombatant like Merton to have written, portraying as hauntingly as he ever did the horrors of war.

The narrator, who is in the foreground of almost every scene, announces to his dumbfounded acquaintances that he has come to England to see the war for himself and to transcribe his reflections in a small diary: "I will keep putting things down," he confides. "until they become clear" (p. 53). His grand themes are guilt and the need for enemies to recognize their common humanity. With respect to the burden of guilt he wants to ascertain how much of the war he himself is responsible for. He accepts responsibility for the conflict partly on semantic grounds — in the sense that he is a person and only persons, not nations, he insists, can bear guilt. In this way Germany is not ultimately responsible for the war, only for beginning it. Little wonder that the New York publishers felt the novel a bit risky in 1941. As a noncombatant, the narrator does not hold himself morally superior to the soldiers (the real Merton felt guilty about entering a monastery when he was on the point of being drafted). War was the soldier's business only in a limited sense. It was essentially a general "retribution for the acts of men," and the narrator, with his remorseful attitude toward his earlier life in Europe, has come to claim his responsibility for the general collapse (p. 118).

The burden of such thoughts gives the narrator a taste for moral pronouncements that make the novel sanctimonious at times. If "you want to identify me," he tells the military police, "ask me not where I live, or what I like to eat, or how I comb my hair, but ask me what I think I am living for, in detail, and ask me what I think is keeping me from living fully for the thing I want to live for. Between these two answers you can determine the identity of any person" (pp. 160-161). A deep thought in a novel groaning under the weight of deep thoughts. What is a modern human being, the narrator asks with rhetorical scorn, but a "collection of objects?" Think of yourself five thousand years from now, he urges earnestly, that same, "unassuming, unimaginative, pathetic, miserly, envious little hypochondriac that you are, dug up as a present to the future" (p. 127). At these points the novel sinks like a stone.

The deep thoughts tend to be more effective when they surface in the reader and when they emerge from the enactment of events than when they are tacked onto the novel by the narrator. The theme of the instinctive unity of all men, for example, is dramatized humorously and tenderly in the scene in which the narrator is given a lift by a truckload of German soldiers on a Normandy road. Thinking he is a Frenchman, the soldiers try to make contact, using the sort of absurd pleasantries that one accumulates in travellers' phrase-books: "Nous ne sommes pas tristes," one of the soldiers says very carefully. "Nous sommes trés heureux." To which the narrator replies with a flourish: "O, bien entendu, vous êtes trés heureux, oui!" . . . The soldier glances at the book. He says sourly: "Pour nous, la vie est un réve. Nous serons toujours jeunes" (p. 171). Merton's theme of the nightmarish war that wastes the youth of the world comes through, and the scene is poignantly realized.

The narrator is effective as well when, instead of moralizing, he attempts to come to terms with the whirlwind generated by the war. His impressions are inevitably filled with the sense of his own awkward isolation, which is Byronic, wistful, and intractable, giving rise to some of the novel's most evocative moments:

> I walk in the midst of the tea-smelling mists, among all the rows of houses in England. I walk among all the brick walls and windows and aspidistras of England, and the sick air smells sweet as a brewery. I look across all the roofs of England, before I knew there was a war. I see the thousands of chimneys in rows, whose smokes lean one way into the mist. (p. 150)

Thematically the narrator's isolation is the basis of his freedom and integrity, as well as of his ability to reach out to others, whatever their political allegiance. Although he travels with an American passport, his country of origin is listed as "Casa." Asked by a British military policeman if he is aware that there is no such country, that Casa is simply a Spanish word meaning "house," he replies coolly: "In my language, Casa means Home" (p. 154). He later links Casa with his being an "amigo de los lirios en el campo"—a friend of the lilies of the field—a clear link with the Gospels and therefore an indication that the narrator's home is not in this world (p. 158). He is thus an "exile all over the earth"

(p. 137). These passages illustrate a coy attraction to allegory on Merton's part, one that leads at times to a certain shallowness in method.

If political allegiances are rejected by the narrator, it is nevertheless clear that an allegiance to Casa does not involve a repudiation of particular places. His recollection of youthful scenes anchors the novel in the concrete world, a welcome relief from the abstractness of many of the novel's introspective vagaries. Some of his youthful friends, he reflects bitterly, were no doubt languishing in German prisons — "wild, disgusted men, standing with their hands in their pockets" and "nearly dead of homesickness for that stony red earth in Languedoc, for those dusty little villages where the farms were all falling to pieces, those hills crazy with zig-zag of vineyard, those red church towers with their harsh bells" (p. 195).

The narrator's "casa," like that of his civilization, lies in idyllic scenes from the past. These scenes recount excursions with his father, brother, and grandparents, such as the celebration of Bastille Day in Dijon that drifts back into his consciousness during his return to French soil: "The high mansards of the hotel flash with the red reflection of the sun, late-setting on the hills full of vines." The medieval city of Dijon is portrayed as "not old," but as speaking with the "clarity and innocence of childhood" (p. 239). The narrator returns to France in order to rekindle the past in his imagination: "I have come back to see the red fermented muck of grape left in the streets when the wine press is taken into the house again, in autumn. I have come to see the provincial ladies drinking grenadine syrup and soda water, . . . at the open air tables under the elm trees in the little towns of the South" (p. 241).

The dramatic pressure of the book arises from the fact that the war presents the narrator with the need to race against time. He plunges into the theater of war in order to see the remnants of his youth before all the evidence is annihilated. In Paris he pauses to consider whether or not he is at the place "where the long black Paris train used to wait in the rain at Boulogne harbor" (p. 237), only to be told by a soldier that it is difficult to tell since the area had been so altered by having been bombed. Hence, the narrator eventually gives up any idea of literally revisiting the scenes of his youth.

The narrator's excursions into the past encompass more than his personal history. It is evident that his "Casa" is also that of the mainstream of Western culture. In Paris, for example, he goes back not only to the city of his youth, with fishermen along the quays and the "long, dark blank wall of the Tuileries," but he travels further back to the Paris of the Impressionists, both the city they lived in and, more significantly, the city that survives eloquently on their canvasses (p. 241):

The wheels of the carriages flickered in the streets like the shimmering of water in the sun. The lungs of the cyclists filled with the smoke and spring of the velod-romes. The oarsmen's girls sang faintly and shyly on the sunny river, where the railway bridges clattered like nickelodeons under the trains de Banlieue.

The skinny shadows of symbolist poets . . . linger in the absinthian green of the Boulevard trees. Under their hats, their pale eyes shine like tea, and their skins are thin as blue-white buttermilk. (pp. 226-227)

The symbol in the novel for the apolitical transmission of civilized values is Madame Gongora, and it is significant that the narrator lives in that lady's "casa." Her house has an urbane, continental atmosphere and in it Madame Gongora is seen drinking coffee and reading the poems of Valéry (p. 73). Through the house are scattered vestiges of the richness of Western culture, including that of Germany — Dresden china, music by Bach, Mozart, and Weber — as well as artifacts from the Greco-Roman culture that fathered Western civilization. This was the world in which Merton grew up and to which he felt he always belonged as he wrote to a friend in 1962 — "pre-war Europe, with its particular heritage and traditional outlook . . . what one might call in a general way Christian humanism."[15]

In a world disfigured by war and steeped in unreality, Madame Gongora's is an "otherworldly" house that helps one to know the "illusion from the truth" (p.188). Madame Gongora, herself, is a sybil who prophesies in macaronic language. The ability of the past to survive the ravages of a world war appears doubtful, but culture turns out to be more resilient than one might expect. The resiliency is symbolized in the small ornate French clock at Madame Gongora's, with its "pair of fancy muses," that had been "stopped by two air raids, and each time repaired" (p. 130).

The unbridled Gothic atmosphere of *My Argument with the Gestapo* is one of the more successful aspects of the novel. London houses have the expression of "patients in a hospital, tired, wondering about themselves, and fearing to be roused from the uneasiness of their secret obsession with disease, by some new, objective alarm, some fresh pain" (p. 50). The face of the infirm city causes the narrator to wonder to himself whether or not it was ever truly healthy. He comes gradually to believe that the elegance and calm, symbolized by the promenading of men in bowler hats and dark suits and carrying rolled-up umbrellas, was an illusion — that the "vast discreet silences of the city were all false" and that the "huge discretion of the fog was hiding everything" (p. 89).

The narrator's reaction to the bombing of London encompasses both horror and relief. The bombs smash the "dirty labyrinth," scattering bricks like "confetti" (p. 19), and the voice of the fire in its "nearness and innocence" talks "happily" to him (p. 24). The flames are innocent in the sense that they rid the city of evil and decay. The conflagration enacts a moral and religious as well as a political and historical process. "I make this journey for the reasons Dante made his," the narrator confides. He had entered the escalator tunnel to the underground (the English name is especially suggestive here), and the tunnel is filled with the sound of a roar "like a barrel full of sea wind." He feels himself "carried downward into the earth" where, below, there are "souls waiting for the boatman Charon, by the black river of hell." At the bottom of the "pit," there are children who wear the "wise, sharp, tired-out faces of old men" (p. 18).

Interiors of buildings resemble labyrinthine tunnels, and walls are hung with "tatters of pictures of bodies, torn out of magazines." Rooms are inhabited by "cold-blooded women with small eyes and metal teeth" (p. 31) and by frightened looking men, all sustaining the air of menace that fills Merton's inferno; through it all there is the sound of the "nightmare-talking" of all London (p. 25). The surrealism is sustained by the air of unreality in the narrator's consciousness that fluctuates distortedly as his mind swims in the "quiet gray water of a half-waking dream" (p. 191). There are occasions when the dream "seeps out" of his ear and his head clears, but these are circumscribed for the reader by an inability to tell which is a better conductor of reality — the dream or the waking.

He inhabits a Kafkaesque universe in which nothing is predictable except fear and in which the appearances of things constantly shift. On the French coast, for example, he is surprised by the calm and afraid that the grass and flowers will sink "like a tide" and give way to the hulks of war, the "skeletons of machines" that he fears lurk in the deep, waving vegetation (pp. 168-169). Similarly, on another occasion, he tenses up in the presence of a German officer who tightens up like a spring, giving no indication what he is going to do next — whether to "break in fifteen pieces like a glass full of boiling tea, or merely burst into tears" (p. 206). The mood of instability is captured definitively in the cocktail bar with its "disturbed" atmosphere — as if the painters and plasterers were working in the next apartment and were going to start in this one tomorrow" (p. 93).

The surrealism proceeds partly from the narrator's neurosis and guilt and partly from the very real destructiveness that roils around him. In spite of the novel's devotion to subjectivism, the bombers overhead, although a source of hallucination in those like the narrator who hide below, are part of a real war. Characteristically though, the external world is metamorphosed, with the narrator seeing the bombers as "copper bees," a recurrent image in his bruised imagination. Early in the novel he hears noises fly out like bees from the windows of buildings that had been smashed by bombs. These hallucinations link him, a non-combatant, with the French soldier late in the novel whose poignant story so vividly conveys the nightmare of war. He too is haunted by unnerving sounds as well as by untreatable skin sores that appear to be emanations from his tormented mind.

The air of menace, hallucination, and self-doubt is not always handled with gravity by Merton, who uses parody to keep the novel from becoming any starker than it already is. Balanced against the grotesques of war is a counter world, a theater of the absurd in which the narrator is a fumbling spy and in which the prevailing standards of reality are those of the popular cinema of the 1920s and 1930s. In hotels the narrator inevitably identifies with movie spies as he dreams about escape and looks for clues to those who are plotting against him. He tears open a letter on the desk in his hotel room to read the following fateful words: "The bearer is under no circumstances to be allowed to leave the Regent Palace Hotel. It is even more important that he never suspect that he has been recognised" (p. 30). Like a celluloid spy, he lands on a deserted section of French beach, having crossed the Channel in a torpedo boat, wearing a Homburg hat, a double-breasted American suit, and brown shoes that never lose their shine.

The film motif symbolizes an ordered world in which meanings are possible. The narrator has spent time at the cinema — as have all contemporary men, Merton believed — seeking in the luminous illusions of the motion picture a respite from an inconsolable loneliness and alienation. The futility of this form of escapism is silhouetted by the garish decorations in the dimly lit theaters, the "gray muses that lolled and smirked on top of the phony arch over the proscenium" and the "horrible balustrades over the top of the proscenium arch, leading into distant nightmarish illusions of impossible Italies full of gypsies and timbrels. Beyond it all, a distant Vesuvius, fabricating smoke" (p. 82).

The novel's dourness is balanced by the crackle of the dialogue and especially by the absurdity of the macaronic language. There is successful satire — as in the characterization of the quixotic Frobisher family, an example of old guard, Yorkshire gentility. With Gilbert and Sullivan on the gramophone and riding horses in the stables, the Frobishers brandish their Kiplingesque doctrine of "duty" with its subdued racial overtones in a manner that causes the narrator to feel that he has stumbled into a "positivistic fairyland." The positivism expresses itself in lessons in utilitarian morality "both reasonable and crude" that are administered to him by Mrs. Frobisher, a woman who had obviously been reading T. H. Huxley with fierce attention (p. 69). She explains patiently on one occasion:

". . . science knows evolution is true. But since religion knows the Bible is true, how can science be true and religion be true?"

It was a question that had never bothered me, but it was a question.

"It is all perfectly simple," she said. "The Book of Genesis merely says in a symbol the same thing that the theory of evolution says in science. The seven days of Genesis are more than likely a symbol for seven hundred thousand or maybe seven million years, I forget which . . ."

She looked at me squarely, having proved her point, and I moved a little uneasily in my chair, and the thought came into my mind: "Maybe this woman is a little crazy." (p. 70)

The macaronic language is a sort of Esperanto, containing most of the languages of Western Europe — including those of the combatants in the war. In this sense it symbolizes the path of unity, cutting across narrow cultural and political borders. This is why it is called the language of Casa. The narrator's journal is a good example of the use of macaronic anti-language. Initially regarded as subversive, the journal is finally written off by the bureaucrats as a collection of "smutty souvenirs" (p. 211). The bureaucrats have a strong distrust of any language that, through its unorthodox form, may, after all, mean something — which is why the narrator is kept so relentlessly under suspicion. There are golden moments in which the odd bureaucrat sees the light, like that in which a British policeman cracks the macaronic code, and his nose suddenly begins to bleed "for awe and misunderstanding" (p. 161). The word "misunderstanding" is Mertonian double-talk, indicating that the policeman has caught on and has begun as a newly liberated man to invent an anti-language of his own. There is ultimately a melancholy futility in the need to resort to this sort of subterfuge, however, and the reader catches a glimpse of this futility when the narrator confesses in an unguarded moment that he wants to die "knowing something besides double-talk" (p. 78).

My Argument with the Gestapo is somewhat erratic in tone and mood, wavering between the prophetic and the absurd, and between the macabre and the boisterous, without allowing the narrative to settle into a single, if complex, view of its elusive subject. Moreover, the book is marred by sanctimoniousness and is weakened at times by Merton's tendency to become overly absorbed in the play of language. In spite of these limitations, however, the novel offers an impressive display of atmospheric and linguistic effects that are tied to a coherent thematic purpose. In so doing it exhibits structural complexities which are remarkable in an early work. Apart from its precocious technical innovations, the book is a moving, impressionistic account of a troubled sensibility in conflict with the idea of war. The war that the narrator confronts is archetypal, and this circumstance gives the novel a somewhat allegorical quality. There is nothing allegorical, however, about the narrator himself, and it is his interior drama that is focal. He emerges, finally, as a sensitively drawn character whose insistent sense of the world as dream becomes a convincing symbol for the traumatic dislocation of war.

While not strictly speaking a novel, *The Seven Storey Mountain* (1948) is nevertheless a formidable narrative. The book was written in a less experimental manner than *My Argument with the Gestapo*, being structured along conventional, chronological lines. The fundamental motif in *The Seven Storey Mountain* is that of a spiritual quest, and the title reflects the arduousness as well as the final success of the journey. The title refers to the interval in which Dante and Virgil had passed through hell to the sea at the foot of the seven-circled mountain of purgatory. The purgatorial theme is amplified by Merton's memory that as a young man he had been blinded by "seven layers of imperviousness," the seven deadly sins which required the refining action of fire.[16]

The book was an unexpected bestseller from the publisher's point of view, although Merton believed it would do well. It had an enormous influence on a whole generation, not only in America but throughout the world. Steeped in religious orthodoxy and scrupulously chaste in tone and outlook, it nevertheless had an impact in some unexpected quarters. Black revolutionary Eldridge Cleaver, for example, was stirred by the book while in Folsom Prison. In spite of Cleaver's rejection of Merton's theism, he found that he "could not keep him out of the room." Most haunting, he felt, was the description of Harlem. "For a while," Cleaver recalled, "whenever I felt myself softening, relaxing, I had only to read that passage to become once more a rigid flame of indignation."[17]

The book had been frequently revised. Merton tried to tone it down partly because of the pressure of Trappist censors, partly because of advice from the publisher, and partly because of his own second thoughts about the text. Some of the excised sections have been reprinted elsewhere, but a question still hangs over the integrity of the text.[18] How much did he, either on his own or at the insistence of others, leave out? There was the girl in Cambridge, for example, who, according to Edward Rice, was on Merton's mind while he was at Columbia. Apparently, she bore Merton's child and was killed along with the child in the Blitz.[19] There is no trace of her in the narrative, although she underlies the scandalized reaction of Merton's guardian at the end of the year at Cambridge.

The original manuscript, which ran to over 600 pages, differs considerably from the published text. One of the early versions is in the possession of Boston College, a copy that Merton described as uncut but that nevertheless reveals large chunks of text removed from an even earlier version. There are sizable omissions in the Boston College manuscript at some tantalizing moments. Standing before some fifth century Byzantine mosaics in Rome, for example, the narrator reflects in this early version: "Someone may wonder why I was able to share the artist's optimism when I stood in the presence of these mosaics being steeped up to the eyes for my own part, in mortal sins."[20] The next eight pages are missing from the manuscript.

Whatever the censors demanded, much of the restraint was imposed by Merton himself. In the early draft, when he approaches the Cambridge section, he confesses that this is the part of the book that he drew back from writing since it involved incidents that were too "dark, and too confused and too dull." He was averse to going over the "drunken evenings and wild parties" that marked that period of his life.[21]

Other passages that failed to make it to the final version were undoubtedly excluded because of their tediousness. A single example from the early manuscript will suffice:

With my eyes open I flung myself into the pursuit of the pleasures and excitements of human love — human love unsatisfied and animal — and by that very fact accepted all the consequences of that dedication, all its accidents, all the other sins that were its results and its companions. Drunkenness, vanity, gluttony, jealousy, envy, pride, detraction and all the variety of species of sins of speech and action and thought, all the day-dreaming and mental adulteries which follow in hundreds of thousands for each single consummated external sin.[22]

One can only endorse Merton's editorial judgment in excising this sort of lugubriousness from the manuscript.

On the other hand, there are places in the early manuscript where one might have liked to see more of the original text retained. Merton's reactions to the sexual drives that tormented him, for example, possess candor and intensity: "No one should allow this tiger to spring on him," he wrote in the early version, "until he is sure that he can immediately possess the elixir that will heal those wounds . . . I went out looking for this particular tiger. For some years I was constantly torn to pieces."[23] Also expunged from the final typescript is an interesting and lengthy discussion of the usefulness to the monk of an earlier experience with love. Merton argued that a knowledge of the kind of love that exists between men and women would help the monk to purify his imagination by allowing him to distinguish natural from mystical love. This was undoubtedly the sort of thing which antagonized the Trappist censors in the late 1940s. It happened to be a view, though, which Merton upheld throughout his life. Writing to a friend in 1966, for example, he said that he did not think a person had "any right to become a monk if he has never fallen in love."[24]

Also excluded from the published text were some verbose polemical passages that had strayed into the narrative. Even though many of these passages were excluded, Merton admitted that he incorporated whole articles into the published text.[25] Thus, the final version is something of a loose, baggy monster, mixing the lyrical, the documentary, the polemical, and the anecdotal. There is a stiffness in his habit of launching chapters with forthright statements that are intended to summarize the moral significance of the part of his life that is about to be described.

The Seven Storey Mountain is splendidly graphic in its presentation of a large gallery of characters. There is, for example, the description of the Extension English class that Merton taught at Columbia. Among those he had to reckon with was a "bad-tempered chemist who was a center of potential opposition because he was taking the course under duress," an "earnest and sensitive Negro youth who sat in the front row dressed in a neat grey suit" peering at Merton intently throughout the class, and the star of the class, a middle-aged lady who had been "taking courses like this for years and who handed in neat and punctilious themes." Finegan, however, outshines them all, sitting "in bewilderment and without promise in one of the back rows," but suddenly blossoming out "with a fecundity in minute and irrelevant material detail." Finegan's copious descriptions of shoe factories made Merton feel as if he were being "buried under fifty tons of machinery" (p. 273). The book is alive with such bright scenes, making it the most picturesque of Merton's works. One of the most memorable scenes involves his waggish friend, Seymour Freedgood, who while editing a military newspaper in India walked into the press room one day where all the typesetters working for him were Hindus — "nice peaceful fellows" — and in full view of all swatted a fly with a report "that rang through the shop like a cannon. Instantly all the Hindus stopped work and filed out on strike" (p. 409).

Merton's narrative perspective attempts to unite the freshness of original experience with the retrospective wisdom of the man who had survived it all. The method works well as long as the older Merton does not overshadow the incidents with interpretive summary so that the vigor and freshness of the younger man are suppressed.

The central, quest motif is interwoven with the theme of identity. Paradoxically, it is made apparent that only when Merton

42

finds out where he belongs will he discover who he is. In America, at Columbia, he had the lingering sense that he was still an Englishman. Similarly, later, in the monastery, he looks back at his earlier self as that of a "stranger," someone who had been "forgotten" (p. 409). Throughout, he is haunted by the problem of his identity, and even as a monk there was "this shadow, this double, this writer" who had followed him into the cloister. Nobody seemed to understand, he reflects gravely, that "one of us has got to die." (p. 410).

The early years show Merton in the company of his itinerant, artistic parents, moving nomadically through France, England, and the United States. While rooted in picturesque fact for the most part, this section rises on occasion to a lyrical pitch: "My father and mother came from the ends of the earth and though they came to stay, they stayed there barely long enough for me to be born" (p. 4). Born in France, he regarded that country as the source of the intellectual and spiritual life of the world to which he belonged, being the country which "grew the finest flowers of delicacy and grace and intelligence and wit and understanding and proportion and taste" (p. 30).

In his preoccupation with identity, Merton selects from the early years those influences that most definitively shaped his character. His discussion of his parents, for example, is marked by this sort of interpretive hindsight: "I inherited from my father his way of looking at things and some of his integrity and from my mother some of her dissatisfaction with the mess the world is in, and some of her versatility" (pp. 3-4). Enforcing the parallels between his own later life as a contemplative/artist and the life of his parents, he describes his parents as being "in the world" but "not of it," since the "integrity of an artist lifts a man above the level of the world without delivering him from it" (p. 3).

Following the untimely death of his mother which, Merton felt, was nonetheless carried off with her characteristic effi-ciency, he went to live in southern France, where his father, an Anglican, enrolled his son in a private Huguenot school. The village of St. Antonin, like many French villages, was so struc-tured that every street "pointed more or less inward to the center of the town, to the Church," a Catholic church naturally and one that had been fitted into the landscape in such a way as to become the "keystone of its intelligibility" (p. 37). In spite of the distrust of monolithic Catholicism that his American grandfather passed on to him, the young Merton drank in a landscape that seemed everywhere to be crowned by old monasteries, and he was always to keep a sense of "those clean, ancient stone cloisters" (p. 6).

In contrast, his feelings about the Calvinistic school he attended were cold. He recalls dreary Sunday mornings gathered around the stove "in the bleak, octagonal edifice which had been erected in one of the courts as a Protestant 'temple' for the students" (p. 53). He disliked as well the social stratification that was implied by the elite school. Even in these early years his deep-seated egalitarian feelings, derived perhaps from the bohemian life-style of his parents, drew him toward what he came to feel was the social universality of Roman Catholicism. He held in retrospect an extraordinary, lifelong affection for a rural Catholic family with which he lived briefly in the Auvergne, a family that humbly but firmly regarded themselves as in the true Church and that regretted tenderly that their young Protestant visitor was not inside with them:

> I gave them the argument that every religion was good: they all led to God, only in different ways, and every man should go according to his own conscience, and settle things according to his own private way of looking at things . . . It was a terrible, a frightening, a very humiliating thing to feel all their silence and peacefulness and strength turned against me, accusing me of being estranged from them, isolated from their security, cut off from their protection and from the strength of their inner life by my own fault. (p. 58)

Merton was drawn not so much to the tenets of their faith as by their warmth and stability, attractive qualities in the eyes of a motherless boy who never quite knew where he was going to move next. Moreover, the family gained luster in his eyes because of the ordinariness of their lives, "sanctified by obscurity, by usual skills, by common tasks, by routine" (p. 56).

His life as an adolescent in Douglaston, Long Island, with his maternal grandparents was as close to normal as his life was ever to become. His grandfather, a zestful Dickensian figure, stormed across his line of vision and stimulated in him an ebullient and passionate attachment to life. The old man was a strong Americanizing influence and possessed a simplicity that was reinforced by a boundless optimism. Merton became conscious of his younger brother John Paul in these years, and retrospectively felt a moral failure in his inability to protect him, a guilty feeling that lasted until John Paul's death in the war in 1943. His earliest memories of his brother are those of exclusion — he playing with the older children while John Paul stands at a safe distance beyond the range of stonethrowing, "as insulted as he is saddened, his eyes full of indignation and sorrow." And yet, Merton recalls with admiration, he did not go away: "The law written in his nature says that he must be with his elder brother, and do what he is doing: and he cannot understand why this law of love is being so wildly and unjustly violated in his case" (p. 23).

John Paul's life turned into a series of uncompleted actions — he never quite graduated from Cornell — he wandered off to Mexico, returning with the back seat of his car full of "records and pictures and strange objects and a revolver and big colored baskets," and he drifted finally into the Second World War before his country had made up its mind to enter that conflict (p. 335). The thought of John Paul gnawed at Merton, who sensed his brother's desultory wanderings as a possible pattern for his own life had he not been fortunate enough to find his way to the contemplative life. Merton's relief at his brother's entry into the Church was as full as it could possibly have been. Preceding the baptism at the monastery, however, he experiences a stab of fear as he imagines John Paul lost within the labyrinth of the abbey. The obsessive image of his brother as haplessly out of reach returns with John Paul standing, confused and unhappy, at a distance which he was "not able to bridge" (p. 398).

The symbolism of John Paul's role is critical to an understanding of the structure of *The Seven Storey Mountain*. For many years John Paul was all that remained of Merton's family, a family whose members gradually died off while Merton was still young.

In addition, John Paul became a perplexing reminder of the world that Merton had left behind him, a world that he could no longer directly involve himself in but to which he still felt profoundly linked by his past and by deep concern. The baptismal scene brings the narrative full circle, recalling the unshakable piety of the peasant family from the Auvergne. Merton had arrived finally at the stability symbolized by that family, and he now found himself looking at his brother as he himself had been looked at before.

The atmosphere of *The Seven Storey Mountain* is heightened by the figure of death stalking throughout the book. The death of Merton's father in England was not only painful but humiliating, the "great helplessness" of the father suddenly falling on his son "like a mountain" (p. 82). In spite of the anguish, his father met death with courage, so that the cancer, which was "pressing him down even into the jaws of the tomb," did not conquer him: "Souls are like athletes," Merton reflects in a memorable passage, "that need opponents worthy of them." His father's battle with the tumor, he felt finally, "was making him great" (p. 83).

The scene became one in which Merton exhibits his penchant for irony of situation, since if the death of his father left the young man depressed for a time, it also had the ironic effect of freeing him, of bringing him out, so that he could follow the movement of his own will, unimpeded by any ties: "I now belonged to the world in which I lived," he recalled. "I became a true citizen of my own disgusting century" (p.85). At Cambridge he set out on a life of debauchery that made him quake in retrospect. At this point the journey motif becomes a descent, a drop into a Dantean abyss: "Shall I follow the circle of the season down into the nadir of winter darkness, and wake up the dirty ghosts under the trees of the Backs, and out beyond the Clare New Building and in some rooms down on the Chesterton Road?" (p. 122)

The darkness is relieved by a brief apparition — that of his father's spirit — in which the young man is forced to look with revulsion at his squandered life. The darkness also lifts on Merton's visit to Rome. He had started out, alone as usual, and with the misconception common to Anglo-Saxons that the real Rome was that of the ancients, whose gray pitted temples were wedged in between the hills and the slums of the city. Fortuitously, he becomes interested in Byzantine mosaics, and their beauty leads him gradually to study the religious subjects that they portray. Thus, without fully realizing what was happening, he became a "pilgrim" (p. 108). The narrative is particularly delicate at this point in tracing the flow of unconscious urgings and conscious desires in the young man as well as in registering the gratitude of the older Merton in looking back at the mystery and fruitfulness of the direction that his life had taken.

The years at Columbia were fertile and restless ones in which Merton tested his abilities and in which his journey seemed more than ever to be leading him to some momentous destiny. This section of the narrative is marked, however, by an atmosphere of false starts and burning decisions. The pace increases considerably, reflecting the energies of a young man approaching the peak of his powers and one who feels increasingly the urgency of a mysterious choice whose terms are not yet clear to him.

As opposed to the classical elegance of Cambridge, Columbia's "big, ugly buildings" were inhabited by rougher, more purposeful students who had little taste for ritual and "no affectations of any kind." Merton felt himself surrounded by a genuine "intellectual vitality" (p. 137). He plunged into his new life with enthusiasm, propelled in part by relief that the dissipation of his life at Cambridge was now behind him. Some of the most evocative description occurs in this phase of the narrative, as it was in this period that Merton began to have a feeling for America—for the land, if not for the civilization reared on it. In the early summer trips to upstate New York he began to get a sense of the "color, and freshness, and bigness, and richness of the land" (p. 200). Later, when he became an instructor at St. Bonaventure University in Olean, he went for long walks, gazing at the snow-covered hills, "white and gold and planted with bare woods, standing out bright against the blinding blue sky," and felt moved to proclaim his love for the continent with its "miles of silences" that God had created for the contemplation of men (p. 310). The American city, on the other hand, became associated in his mind with the *Inferno* and was symbolized by the morgue at Bellevue with its rows of refrigerated corpses — the drowned, the drunk, the addicts, the paupers, the suicides—the bodies of those who had "died of contemporary civilization" (p. 153). The symbolic polarity of city and wilderness became deeply embedded in Merton's consciousness at this time.

The description of the trip to Cuba is a pivotal one in terms of the book's structure. Merton's feeling for Latin America was a reflection of his cosmopolitanism and of his instinct to reach out to others, particularly those who were physically and culturally different from himself. In Cuba he entered joyfully into the religious and social ritual of the towns, mixing gregariously into the *paseo*, a promenade in which the whole town participated, and making friends with many of those who passed by. The reader perceives that he liked ritual after all — if not the subdued rites of Cambridge, then the more earthy and passionate rituals of Cuban society and religion. During the Mass in the cathedral in Havana he becomes ecstatic as he is blinded suddenly by the "manifestation of God's presence" (p. 284). There would be no turning back.

Merton was in the homestretch, although he did not realize it at the time, and this circumstance adds to the dramatic interest of this section of the book. He was headed up his heavenly mountain, but was confused by what seemed to him to be a myriad of choices. He could become a teacher at St. Bonaventure's, dedicating himself to God in an informal manner as a layman; he rejected this choice as too secure and bland. He tried the Franciscans, but became hopelessly entangled over that decision. In addition, he was tempted to work with the Baroness de Hueck at Friendship House in Harlem. "Here in this huge, dark, steaming slum," he wrote, "hundreds of thousands of Negroes are herded together like cattle, most of them with nothing to eat and nothing to do . . . In this huge cauldron, inestimable natural gifts, wisdom, love, music, science, poetry are stamped down and left to boil with the dregs of an elementally corrupted nature, and thousands upon thousands of souls are destroyed by vice and misery and degradation, obliterated, wiped out, washed from the register of the living, dehumanized" (p. 345). Stunned by what he had seen, he felt compelled to do what he could. To add to his already lengthy list of options, he was drafted.

His life had all been decided earlier, however, although he

either did not realize it or could not believe it. He had made a retreat at the Abbey of Gethsemani in the spring of 1941 during Holy Week, and if his consciousness in the months ahead was bewildered by the choices confronting it, his subconscious had already decided. In Olean, New York, he had an extrasensory experience that decided it — he heard "the great bell of Gethsemani," hundreds of miles away, "ringing in the night" (p. 365). Skeptical of the incident — though steadied by it — he became convinced that the bell was telling him where he belonged.

Bursting with vigor, he found himself suddenly craving the anonymity of the contemplative life and envying the cenobitic lives of those who were "lost in the picture," as he put it (p. 317). His journey is pictured as toward darkness, the darkness of the great mystics and of the presence of God. Within the monastic community he would journey forward in age and into the blankness that he had observed in the older monks.

Finally resolved, Merton approaches his destination with ecstatic anticipation. His impressions as he nears the monastery late in the evening constitute one of the most vivid and evocative passages in the book:

> I looked at the rolling country, and at the pale ribbon of road in front of us, stretching out as grey as lead in the light of the moon. Then suddenly I saw a steeple that shone like silver in the moonlight, growing into sight from behind a rounded knoll. The tires sang on the empty road, and, breathless, I looked at the monastery that was revealed before me as we came over the rise. At the end of an avenue of trees was a big rectangular block of buildings, all dark, with a church crowned by a tower and a steeple and a cross: and the steeple was as bright as platinum and the whole place was as quiet as midnight and lost in the all-absorbing silence and solitude of the fields. Behind the monastery was a dark curtain of woods, and over to the west was a wooded valley, and beyond that a rampart of wooded hills, a barrier and a defence against the world. (p. 320)

The pastoralism is characteristic of the lyrical mood that pervades the final section of the narrative. Set among the Kentucky
hills, Gethsemani holds the contemplative in close contact with
nature. Merton perceived that his vocation was not only to the
contemplative life but to this very place. He felt that he had
arrived at the "real capital" of the country, the "center of all the
vitality" that is in America and the "cause and reason why the
nation is holding together" (p. 325).

The closing of *The Seven Storey Mountain* is dominated by the
cycle of the seasons and by the young monk's blissful entry into
them and into contact with the God whom he felt to be matrix of
all nature. The pace of the narrative slows in harmony with the
procession of natural forms. Things settle into a soft light as the
monks go about their work in the fields, a work that is beautifully
attuned to the events of the liturgical year. In Advent the monks
file out with mattocks to dig up briars. The trees are "stripped
bare" in an austerity that symbolically parallels that of the penitential season. In Paschal time the cowled monks go out to the
fields to plant peas and beans, paralleling the rebirth that is
symbolized in the Easter liturgy. In the warm months they go out
with straw hats on their heads to hay, and then later on to harvest
the crops in the early autumn of "bright, dry days, with plenty of
sun, and cool air, and high cirrus clouds" when the trees have
turned "rusty and blood color and bronze along the jagged hills"
(p. 399). The style is especially fervid in this section as Merton's
imagination settles serenely upon a world he finds he has every
reason to love.

In spite of its occasional didacticism *The Seven Storey Mountain*
has through its marshalling of some major symbols and themes
an impressive cumulative power. Moreover, Merton shows his
considerable skill in narrative structuring throughout the book.
If one of the difficulties with his earlier narratives had been their
unresolved endings and arbitrary arrangement, he clearly made
a different job of *The Seven Storey Mountain,* whose organization
is both lucid and dramatically satisfying. Furthermore, his handling of the details of characterization and incident is much
firmer and more vivid in *The Seven Storey Mountain* than in *My
Argument with the Gestapo.* The stimulus of real experience appears to have been of benefit, as opposed to the hypothetical

situation he portrayed in *My Argument with the Gestapo*. Rooting himself in his own evolving story, he managed to create a memorable book. In spite of the sweeping changes in social history which have taken place since the book was originally published, it continues to attract new readers, possibly because in addition to being an absorbing spiritual autobiography it is also a reminder in a period dominated by statism of the flourish of individual destiny.

Notes

[1]Robert Giroux, "Thomas Merton 1915-1968," in *Columbia College Today*, XV (1969), p. 69.
[2]Ibid., p. 69.
[3]Naomi Burton-Stone, *No More Sentinels* (New York, 1964), p. 238.
[4]Giroux, "Thomas Merton 1915-1968," p. 69.
[5]Ibid., p. 69.
[6]Naomi Burton-Stone, "A Note on the Author and This Book," in *My Argument with the Gestapo* by Thomas Merton (New York, 1969), pp. 9-10.
[7]Letter to Mark Van Doren, Sept. 19, 1946.
[8]Letter to James Laughlin, June 27, 1968.
[9]Letter to Suzanne Butorovich, Feb. 11, 1968.
[10]Letter to Mark Van Doren, March 12, 1968.
[11]*My Argument with the Gestapo* (New York, 1969), p. 6. Subsequent references will be incorporated in the text.
[12]*The Seven Storey Mountain* (New York, 1948), p. 336.
[13]Notebook #88. The entry is dated December, 1967.
[14]*The Sign of Jonas* (New York, 1953), p. 321.
[15]Letter to Joost Am Meerloo, Nov. 4, 1962.
[16]*The Seven Storey Mountain*, pp. 122-123. Subsequent references will be incorporated in the text.
[17]*Soul on Ice* (New York, 1968), p. 34.
[18]These were edited by Sister Therese Lentfoehr, to whom Merton sent most of his early manuscripts, and they included the following: "First Christmas at Gethsemani," *Catholic World*, CLXX (1949), pp. 166-173; "Todo y Nada: Writing and Contemplation," *Renascence*, II (1950), pp. 87-101; "I Will Be Your Monk," *Catholic World*, CLXXI (1950), pp. 86-93; and "Thomas Merton on Renunciation," *Catholic World*, CLXXI (1950), pp. 420-429.

[19]*Man in the Sycamore Tree,* p. 19.
[20]"The Seven Storey Mountain," Boston College manuscript, p. 209.
[21]Ibid., p. 223.
[22]Ibid., p. 173.
[23]Ibid., p. 162.
[24]Letter to Thomas Congdon, Sept. 25, 1966.
[25]Letter to Jacques Maritain, Feb. 10, 1949.

Diarist

AS OPPOSED TO THE NARRATIVE writings, which depict the lives of a group of characters in a formal structure, the journals focus introspectively on a single, interior life and are quite informal in style. It was in his journals that Merton came closest in a verbal medium to the spontaneous self-expression that he achieved in his calligraphies. The diaries are fresh and candid, fragmentary and loosely ordered yet more incisive than any of his other writing. Their great quality, though, is their immediacy, so that even some of those incidents that are related vividly in the novels and sketches are presented with a more convincing directness in the journals. Merton believed that in his journals he communicated things that "could never be said in any other way."[1]

If the narratives and poems are primarily imaginative and the essays mainly expository, the journals are bound by no such categories. They are completely heterogeneous, brimming with bits of poems and prayers, aphoristic observations, lyrical interludes, anecdotes, the documenting of the daily round, and his candid assessment of his spiritual progress. The emphasis is always existential, always on the things that have been absorbed through experience. The essays, on the other hand, concern themselves primarily with his intellectual grasp of the world around him.

It would be naive to argue that Merton was unself-conscious in his journals; either he or his superiors always had an eye on the possible publication of everything he ever wrote. The published journals were carefully edited versions of Merton's holographic diaries. At the same time, he was obviously more naked in the pages of the journals than anywhere else. Although there are private diaries of Merton's that will not be published for some years, as well as public ones that either have been published or will be published, a look at his papers reveals that he left diary entries, sometimes of an extremely personal nature, almost anywhere. One encounters these especially in his notebooks, where he would often apply the things that he was reading to his own situation. It was almost as if in his determination to open himself to other men he wanted to leave important, personal messages about himself where they could not help but be found.

Merton had a habit of writing down whatever fortuitously drifted through his mind. In this connection John Howard Griffin has made the acute observation that Merton "allowed himself to be saturated by an awareness of the reality of each moment, listening always for what it had to tell him."[2] If it was not something that swam into his line of vision, it was often the surfacing of a stray memory. His habit was to recover it, get it on paper, whether or not it would ever be of use. He seems to have had an almost Proustian sense that you are what you remember. The journals were the fountainhead of all of his other writings. Ideas often saw first light there before being transposed into essay, poem, or narrative.

The four published journals fall into four periods in Merton's life, each capturing his interests at that time as well as reflecting his development as a diarist. The *Secular Journal* (1959) covers the early years, from 1939 to 1941, the restless and nomadic period that immediately preceded his entry into the monastery. It is difficult to ascertain how much value he placed upon his first published journal. He described his first journal as containing the "callous opinions and all the other defects"[3] of youth, and while he appears to have seen a certain charm in the book, he did not take it seriously enough to include it among the list of his books that he drew up in 1967, a list in which he assessed two other journals — *The Sign of Jonas* and *Conjectures of a Guilty Bystander* — as among his best works.

The most paradoxical aspect of the *Secular Journal* is its title. While it deals with the author's pre-monastic years, it seems anything but secular in tone. One of the book's reviewers wrote that the central character was already in the abbey, psychologically, if not in fact, a young man who wore his crepe-soled shoes like sandals, whose belt "had begun to suggest a cincture," and whose eyes were "already in custody."[4] The young Merton seems to have felt this himself as he drifted through social gatherings in the company of young women who, he thought, had him "figured for a priest."[5]

Much of the journal is a sort of commonplace book, containing Merton's reflections on his reading and on the shaping of events around him. His reflections on Breughel's painting of the wedding dance is a good example of the entries in the *Secular Journal*. He notices first the "pyramidal" arrangement of those in the dance, set against barns and sheds, and surmounted by two couples who were "drawn as flat as Thurber pictures." Suddenly there emerges "like the keystone of the whole picture, one, rigid, solitary, little man in grey with his back to the whole business, simply looking away at nothing, off at the back and top of the picture." In discovering this little man, his eye is led to a barn full of people whom he had completely missed up to that point (pp. 17-18). Apart from the attractiveness to Merton of anyone who happened to be looking in a direction in which others were not looking, he becomes aware here of Breughel's creation as a mysterious world filled with subtle directional signals. The description of the painting is typical of Merton's art as a diarist. It is freshly drawn from immediate experience, and it focuses with elaborate concentration on that experience in a way that would not occur given greater perspective and more time for reflection. His journal entries magnify the moment, separating it from the stream of life perhaps, but also revealing the richness of its detail and the unfolding of its otherwise hidden and transient significance.

While ruminations about war, Hitler, and the burden of guilt seem to obscure the moment by losing it in secondhand speculation, the moment revives, so to speak, in some reflections on the war. One of these involves Merton's impressions of a German propaganda film. The film showed razed buildings, blasted bridges, wrecked trains, piles of captured guns "and other nondescript stuff" along with views of a sleek German army in which the men appeared to be "nothing but more equipment." The picture included an "obscene" shot in which a bomber released a stick of bombs, "like some vile beetle laying eggs in the air, or dropping its filth." With inexplicable oversight, he observes, the German censors failed to cut from the film the face of a soldier whose fatigue and dismay undercut the whole thrust of the propagandists' message: "Great rings surrounded his eyes which were full of exhaustion, pain and protest. And he kept staring, turning his head and fixing his eyes on the camera as he went by demanding to be seen as a person, and not as the rest of the cattle" (pp. 127-130). Such moments give the *Secular Journal* its vitality and its particular interest as the record of a sensitive young man's impressions at a critical point in history.

There are two other scenes in the *Secular Journal* which are worth noting. The first occurs during Merton's trip to Cuba in the spring of 1940, the second, a year later, during his retreat at the Abbey of Gethsemani in Kentucky. The journey to Cuba was a charmed one, from the moment of his first view of Havana with the city emerging with the "color of a pearl" from the morning haze (p. 53). The city, with its throb of life, overwhelmed him with its "brilliance and the lights and the shadows and the noise and the cries and the colors and the smells and the tremendous vitality that flows in and out of the big iron gates of the dark patios, and in and out of the dark shops that stand open to the street" (p. 56). Havana was not only an exotic stimulus to his imagination, but a vantage point from which he could look back at America.

It was, he decided, more of a genuine city than New York because it was not its buildings that were important, but rather the abundance of its life:

> Negroes with cigars in their mouths and great bloody aprons, carrying huge sides of beef out of trucks and into dark cavernous butcher shops that open right out on the narrow street. Clusters and clusters of bananas and papayas and coconuts and God knows what different kinds of fruits hanging up in the fruiterers'. Piles of cigarettes, shelves and shelves of books, cigars, medicines, sheets and sheets of numbered lottery tickets hanging up over a tobacconist's counter, and more magazines than I ever saw at once in my life: dozens of newspapers. (pp. 56-57)

What made Havana superior to New York was not its spirituality, but, paradoxically, its materialism. New York lived amidst abstractions and geometric buildings. Its wealth was almost intangible, hidden in "account books full of figures and ledgers and fancy printed stocks and ticker tape and nervous energy and electricity" (p. 57). The wealth of Havana, on the other hand, could be seen, touched, and tasted. It was suited, therefore, to the nature of the people who lived in the city as well as to the wandering tourist who found his senses refreshed in merely strolling through it.

The spring retreat at Gethsemani, which was to decide Merton's future, is equally memorable. His senses and mind were at a high pitch throughout the Holy Week liturgy, and the entries at this time are succinct and keen: "This is the feast of our treachery," he wrote on Good Friday — the "rattle makes its terrible clatter in the cloister. The tabernacle is empty and lies open. It is as though the winds of death blew right through us" (p. 200). He found solace in the Kentucky countryside. The Kentucky spring burst open for him, speaking of survival and renewal at the same time as the liturgy enacted its drama of death and defeat:

> The sun today was as hot as Cuba. Tulips in the front garden have already opened their chalices too wide and have gone blowsy. The bees were at work, one in each flower's cup, although it is still only April. Apple trees are in blossom, and every day more and more buds come out on the branches of the tall trees of the avenue before the gatehouse.
>
> Trappist brothers in their medieval hoods, and heavy home-made boots, tramp along in a line through the vineyard. Bells ring in the steeple. (p. 198)

Each of the journals has its distinctive effect. The *Secular Journal*, perhaps because it is an early work, has an appealing ingenuousness. It evokes the passion, vigor, and optimism of youth as well as the luxury of time conferred by youth through which many different kinds of experience may be tried out.

The Sign of Jonas (1953) is Merton's second journal. It is one of his finest works as well as being a masterpiece of its kind in twentieth century letters. It covers his life in the monastery from

1946 to 1952. It was edited so that it might not suffer too severely from the fragmentation and arbitrariness inherent in the diarist's mode. The title that he gave the journal reflects his attempt to impose a formal structure upon informal materials, and the contents of his recorded experience during this period may have been especially helpful to him in this respect. His life at this time was extremely sheltered; he lived literally as well as psychologically enclosed within the ordered world of the abbey, and although his was not a life without stress, his outlook appears to have been more stable during this period than in any other part of his life. It is this stability that gives *The Sign of Jonas* its satisfying underlying unity.

The title exhibits an important symbol in Merton's thinking about himself, the sign of his deliverance from a helpless and doomed world. Travelling inside the whale meant travelling within the "belly of a paradox," that of the awesome rising of life from the dead.[6] The symbol of the whale is most emphasized in the final section of the journal, "The Fire Watch," in which Merton is enveloped in darkness. At this point, the darkness of the whale merges symbolically with the darkness of God. A problem, he wrote, is that it "is the whale we cherish," by which he meant man's life and freedom, here and now. The whale must die, though, for the cycle of resurrection to be fulfilled. If not, "the inevitable will come to pass," a fatalistic repetition of the cycle with the swallowing of Jonas by the whale all over again — so that life "will be swallowed again in death and its last state will be worse than the first" (p. 341). There is no hatred for the whale, which symbolizes nature. Nevertheless, man must escape from the whale for his own survival, and the whale must inevitably die — while man slips into "the clear, busy with his orisons, clothed and in his right mind, free, holy and walking on the shore" (p. 341).

The underlying tone of the book is ascetic, although the mood is soft and effusive. The tension between tone and mood is one of the secrets of the book's dramatic energy. The tone is that of a man who, like Jonas, is censorious about the world he has escaped, a world that he sees as bent on self-annihilation:

Sooner or later the world must burn, and all things in it—

all the books, the cloister together with the brothel, Fra Angelico together with the Lucky Strike ads which I haven't seen for seven years because I don't remember seeing one in Louisville. Sooner or later it will all be consumed by fire and nobody will be left — for by that time the last man in the universe will have discovered the bomb capable of destroying the universe and will have been unable to resist the temptation to throw the thing and get it over with. (p. 122)

Set against this apocalyptic vision is the idyllic mood sustained by Merton's deep happiness. The five years since he entered Gethsemani had "gone by like five weeks" (p. 17). While the ascetic in him perceives the final destruction of the world with indifference, the contemplative and artist embrace the days with love and feel a pang of regret at the passing of each day:

Another August had ended and we will never see it again. It was hot and stuffy all day, but although it did not rain, after Vespers the air was cooler and the sky had brushed up to look something like September. O frightening and beautiful month with Saint Giles standing in your door to be the patron of those who are afraid. Soon we will fight the fields of corn.

We have the biggest retreat of the year. There are eighty-two or more in the guest house that was build for fifty. One of them is an old man with a magnificent white beard and a big curled mustache. He must be one of the wonders of Kentucky and I am overwhelmed with awe whenever he appears. (pp. 61-62)

The journals derive much of their charm from Merton's conversation with himself. This conversation is the diarist's idiom, containing the liveliness of speech which one finds in a play or a novel, while holding to the purpose of focusing on the interior life of a single narrator:

Rain. It is cold. Everyone's getting colds, including Father Ignatius Smith, O.P., who is preaching to us. I bet his brother is a Police Captain. All retreats do me good. And this one too. Conferences simple, hard-boiled, and sometimes very loud. If his brother is not a cop, I'll settle for a football coach. But he does me good.

After having doctors and sisters telling me for three weeks to rest and take care of myself it is a relief to have someone roar at the whole community about idleness and timidity. "If you are worn out," he says, "you are just getting off to a good start." (p. 315)

In addition to the peaceful humor that pervades the passage, Merton's comment that all retreats did him good reflects the underlying mood of acceptance that is characteristic of the whole book, a mood that is absent in the other journals.

More than in any of the other journals, *The Sign of Jonas* gives one a sense of the ordinary routine of the contemplative's life. Merton liked the physical work, even though it was arduous and his health uncertain. The summer heat was hard on the fully clothed monks, as he revealed in an entry for July 18, 1948:

Very hot. The birds sing and the monks sweat and about 3:15 when I had just changed all our clothes for the fourth time today and hung out the wet ones to dry, I stood in the doorway of the grand parlor and looked at a huge pile of Kentucky cumulus cloud out beyond Mount Olivet — with a buzzard lazily planing back and forth over the sheep pasture, very high and black against the white mountain of cloud. Blue shadows on the cloud. (p. 111)

Brimming with idealism he anticipated the nights in the community when "we stand in our boiling tunnel and shout our *Salve* at the lighted window you feel the whole basilica swing with the exultation of the monks and brothers who are dissolving in this humid furnace" (p. 204).

Excluded from the inner sanctum of those who were given

skilled physical work, he sometimes felt bemused at the sight of such work. In one scene he observed his fellow monks on the roof making exhaust holes in order to insert some new fans, leaving two novices below near the doorways with signs that read "Falling Bricks." Ironically, he noted, "one of them was standing at the precise spot where all the falling bricks would land on his head. He was saying the rosary in an attitude of perfect abandonment" (p. 205).

One of the major themes of *The Sign of Jonas* is that of Merton's newly found sense of identity within the community of comtemplatives. He was convinced that he had done the right thing, that he was meant to be where he was, and he felt a warm kinship with his community: "I am part of Gethsemani," he wrote, "I belong to the family" (p. 32). He felt his closeness to the community so profoundly in this period of life that it produced some surprising adjustments in his outlook. Controversy, for example, which earlier in his life he seemed to thrive on now became "Oppressive beyond measure" (p. 42). The reason was that in the abbey's climate of silence no one could answer back. "After years of being unable to talk back," he observed, "a Cistercian is apt to be nauseated by the mere suggestion of controversy. When a conference is really argumentative the atmosphere gets to be so tense that the monks cannot even seek solace by falling asleep. When it is all over they file out in silent dejection, dispersing, running outdoors on every side to find solitude and fresh air" (pp. 42-43).

As Merton sank his roots into the soil of Gethsemani, the monastery became more and more lustrous in his eyes. He loved to go up into the woods and look back at Gethsemani, which he felt "made much more sense in its surroundings" (p. 201). The beauty of Gethsemani did not come from its buildings. It was the spirit of the men within that continually shaped scenes for him, such as the sight of a monk painting the cross on one of the steeples with yellow traffic paint. The painter became fixed in Merton's imagination, swinging "up there for days in the sky with his angel holding on to him. (He upset a bucket of paint and I could see it flying upside down on the end of the rope, and the paint turned to spray before it was half way down, and a drop fell on our Psalter and there were little yellow spots all over the stones and the bushes of the cemetery where today I saw a hawk" (p. 123).

At this period of his life Merton saw the questions of identity and community as beautifully intertwined. He became convinced that, in spite of the self-effacement implicit in the life of his community, "our duty is to be more ourselves, not less."[7] In addition, he felt at this time that the stability of the life within the monastery was fundamental to this growth in self-identity. Taking up the major symbol of the book, he wrote that the vow of stability through which he became rooted in a particular community and place had been for him "the belly of the whale" (p. 10).

As he identified with Gethsemani, he also came to feel centrifugally his identity as a Kentuckian and an American. He had already come to love the Kentucky countryside, but now he included Louisville: "I feel, very dutifully, that Louisville is my city. Why? Well, it is the place I go to when I say 'I am going to town.' The fact that I practically never leave the monastery to go 'in town' makes no difference whatever" (p. 310). As for America, he had become a citizen in 1951 and embraced his country "atomic bomb and all," feeling it curious that nationality should finally come to have a significance for him since he had lived for thirty-six years without one (p. 323).

At the same time, Merton's isolation from the world is one of the book's principal themes. He felt it wrap itself around his fellow monks, noticing that the bulk of the Christmas mail went to the recent arrivals while those who had come long ago received almost nothing. Although he was somewhat dismayed by the growing number of letters that were sent to him after the publication of The Seven Storey Mountain, he maintained his solitude more effectively than he felt capable of doing in later life. Unlike later journals, The Sign of Jonas contains very little reference to or sign of interest in outside events. The outside world seemed to impinge very little on Merton — a small plane crash near the abbey — an amusing confrontation with some hunters observed poaching on the monastery's lands — were about all.

The incident involving the hunters is an amusing and urbane study in self-consciousness and is one of Merton's best anecdotes. In the winter of 1950 he had been sitting by the old horsebarn looking down at the pasture when he sighted a couple of hunters: "White pants and brown pants." They were not serious hunters, he decided, because they seemed to be talking continuously. The dog ran ahead of them barking, and it seemed as little serious about the hunt as its owners. Suddenly, one of the hunters climbed up onto the monastery's enclosure wall, ostensibly to have a better shot at any passing rabbits. "It was all an act," Merton reflected: "The whole universe knew that as soon as he fired the gun he would fall off the wall backwards inside the enclosure, perhaps into the dirty old bathtub full of rain water and spring water and green weeds which is placed there as a horsetrough." Then, he added waggishly, "he would have to become a monk" (pp. 264-265).

Meanwhile, he wondered whether or not his own position had become equivocal. Perhaps he was supposed to resent the intrusion by the hunter upon the monastery's stillness and to wave the man off silently. He resolved to sit still with his reading so that the hunter would not become aware of him—and yet should the hunter perceive that he had been observed, he would infer that Merton "entertained toward him and the universe he represented an abstract, disembodied, and purely official good will" (p. 265). Nothing happened. Not a shot was fired: "I did not turn a page of the book I may or may not have had with me. Not a drop of rain fell. Not a bird sang. Ours is a comfortable world," he concluded wistfully, "without either science or wisdom" (p. 265). The inherent narrative value of the incident is skillfully drawn out, creating a droll study of cloistered shyness and vigilance.

In order to underline the extent of his isolation from the world, Merton presents a series of tableaux drawn from dreams. One of those involves a junk wagon that he had seen in Louisville on a couple of occasions. The wagon comes back to him in a dream, complete with the bells of the mule that pulled it ringing in his ears and the brass disks glittering in the sun: "The green boards held themselves together by miracle in their marvelous disorder. But now the junk man's wife was driving; the junk man walked behind" (pp. 317-318). The image coalesces in Merton's mind with Gray Street in Louisville, on which he had seen a "black carnival mask with broken elastic lying in the dirty snow" in front of one of the old ornate houses (p. 318). The dimming images of the city further coalesce in his mind into a "mist of melting snow," symbolic of the way in which he perceived the outside world, a world about which he was only certain that he was "not part of it" (p. 318).

The delicacy of Merton's response to nature is an important source of the eloquence of *The Sign of Jonas:*

> Yesterday there was snow again and wind froze ribs on top of the drifts along the hillsides; sun shone through the copper grass that grew above the snow on Saint Joseph's hill, and it looked as if the snow was all on fire. There were jewels all over the junk the brothers dumped out there where the old horsebarn used to be. A bunch of old worn-out window-screens were lying about and they shone in the sun like crystal. (p. 317)

As Merton had felt in his reservations about art, there was always the possibility that nature would seduce his attention with its inexhaustible fecundity and its suggestive ability to link up with other kinds of experience. A little locust tree, for example, which had died and "spilled all the fragments of its white flowers over the ground," became associated in his mind with the painting of Seurat (p. 49). Winter mornings were especially suggestive, the sky filled with small high clouds that looked like "ice-floes, all golden and crimson and saffron, with clean blue and aquamarine behind them, and shades of orange and red and mauve down by the surface of the land where the hills were just visible in a pearl haze and the ground was steel-white with frost — every blade of grass as stiff as wire" (p. 137). The exquisite detail of these descriptions is evidence that Merton, like his father, had the painter's eye. Moreover, he tried to turn the details of the landscape to contemplative use in order to achieve the elusive *inscape* that he admired in Hopkins, the tracing of the detail of the structure of natural objects under the pressure of an inspired intuition so that the spectator eases himself into the center of the object he is looking at. In so doing he does not disturb the integrity of that object and becomes able to "see the thing from the very point where it springs from the creative power of God."[8]

The luminous quality that was always part of Merton's vision of nature was associated with its wildness and purity. The pristine character of the wilderness was a mirror of those same paradisal qualities and energies he perceived in man but that had atrophied because of the deadening effect of civilization. The meandering and spontaneous action of nature pointed emblematically in fact to the creative and spontaneous energies that were latent within all of being. Nature was not necessarily kind, however, as the incident of the hawk and the starlings indicates. Having settled down after having been frightened by an eagle, the starlings move about on the ground, singing. Suddenly, a "scare" goes into the "cloud" of birds and they rise off the ground. A hawk swoops down and flies "straight into the middle of the starlings" just as they are getting off the ground. They rise into the air and there is a slight scuffle on the ground as the hawk gets his "talons into the one bird he had nailed" (p. 274). Merton ponders the Darwinian character of the scene: "It was a terrible and yet beautiful thing, that lightning flight, straight as an arrow, that killed the slowest starling" (p. 275). The scene was made more significant for him by the behavior of the hawk, which did not fly off with its prey, but stayed in the field "like a king," taking his time in eating his prey. "I tried to pray, afterward," Merton writes. "But the hawk was eating the bird." He was not so much repelled as awed, feeling finally that the hawk should be studied by "saints and contemplatives; because he knows his business" (p. 275). The consolation of nature, therefore, did not lie in its tenderness but rather in its capacity to symbolize reality. The symbolism of the hawk and of the whale hangs over the latter part of *The Sign of Jonas* as stirring emblems of nature's mysterious power and beauty. Nevertheless, Merton portrays nature as ultimately doomed. Consequently, the resourceful pilgrim will permit himself to be carried by the whale, by nature, to some other place, to look not only at the beauty of nature but through it. Otherwise, Merton's symbolic construct implies, one will suffer the fate of the starlings.

The Sign of Jonas culminates in a remarkable section called "The Fire Watch" in which Merton walks through the monastery as night watchman, reliving as he does so some of the past scenes of his life there. The two major symbols are those of darkness and the whale. The community is pictured as a "holy monster," and the monks are portrayed as "packed in the belly of the great heat" (p. 349). The enveloping night resounds with "animal eloquence," while the earth, which the whale symbolizes throughout, is seen to relax and slowly cool "like a huge wet living thing" (p. 350). The sequence ends appropriately with dawn, lustrous with "drops of dew that show like sapphires in the grass as soon as the great sun appears," a timeless moment in which all that has been implicit in Merton's apocalyptic vision of the whale resolves itself into a divine utterance: "I have always overshadowed Jonas with My mercy, and cruelty I know not at all" (p. 362).

The ocean of darkness that envelops this section of *The Sign of Jonas* is used as a paradoxical symbol throughout the book. The darkness does not convey the sinister connotations conventionally implied by this symbolism. Instead it bathes the mind and awakens it to new life after the attrition of the day: "Baptized in the rivers of night, Gethsemani has recovered her innocence. Darkness brings a semblance of order before all things disappear" (p. 349). Darkness is the belly of the whale, a warm and protective natural world in which, contrary to the confusion of cities, one finds clarity and calm.

The journey through the darkness of the whale is not only a journey into the mystery of being but also a journey within so that on his nocturnal rounds Merton finds himself face to face with his past and with the enigma of his life. His journey through the darkness is not only through distance, therefore, but through time as well. He encounters not only the phantoms of his own past but those of his historic monastery, and he comes to feel "like an archeologist suddenly unearthing ancient civilizations" (p. 354). The imagery reinforces the symbolism of darkness as a paradoxical source of vision—the darkness helps him to see things that he would not otherwise be able to see.

Darkness conventionally symbolizes death, but here it symbolizes life and renewal. Moving through the old guest house, now empty, Merton feels the darkened house to be like a "sick person who has recovered. This is the Gethsemani that I entered," he writes, "whose existence I had almost forgotten" (p. 357). In a symbolic "ascent" of the old monastery tower he finds himself paradoxically descending into the past in walking on stairs that went "back beyond the civil war." He thinks of himself as climbing to the top of a "religious city, leaving its modern history behind" (p. 359). The emotional resonance of the section derives from his imaginative attempt to establish contact with the deepest roots of his community — a return to sources which enables him to experience the continuity and meaning of his own history.

The way back through the darkness was also symbolically the way out of the self. At a certain point, Merton writes, it was possible for the spirit to leave the "purple" fish of the mind's relaxed contemplation and to enter a world where everything was "charged with intelligence, though all is night," a world in which the "holy cellar" of one's mortal existence "opens into the sky. It is a strange awakening," he adds, "to find the sky inside you and beneath you and above you and all around you so that your spirit is one with the sky, and all is positive night" (pp. 339-340).

Conjectures of a Guilty Bystander (1965) covers the busy period from 1956 to 1965 when Merton was Master of Novices and is a very different book from *The Sign of Jonas*, lacking the intimacy of the earlier work and being far more discursive. It is characterized, however, by the same lithe conversational idiom that marks all of the journals. The entries are not dated, reflecting the rearrangement of the material, so that, presumably, the ideas contained could more easily attach themselves to one another without the distractions of a formal chronological framework.

The book differs greatly in mood and rhythm from the other journals, although its rapid pace anticipates the *Asian Journal*. Reflecting the increased tempo of his life, Merton's journal during this period became almost telegraphic at times, resulting sometimes in a fortuitous effect: "Hawk. First the shadow flying downward along the wall of sunlit foliage. Then the bird itself, trim, compact substance, in the sky overhead, quite distinct from woods and trees, flying in freedom. Barred tail, speckled wings, with sunlight shining through them."[9] The concentrated brevity of such descriptions gave rise to an attractive haiku effect. The descriptions of birds are especially memorable: "Flycatchers, shaking their wings after the rain" (p. 125).

If *Conjectures of a Guilty Bystander* could be said to have a central theme, it is that of exploration. While he was in the process of exploring his links with the world outside, Merton found himself looking more and more critically at his community. His viewpoint is often sardonic and censorious, a contrast to the soft effusiveness of *The Sign of Jonas*. The mercurial tone is amplified by the dark and restless mood and by the discursive structure.

These were years of change. Merton was growing older, more philosophical perhaps, and yet with a gnawing realization that he had not yet after all found his niche. He felt increasingly suffocated by the way in which his life had become intertwined with the institutionalized routine of his community, and his old passion to live the life of a solitary returned with greater force than ever. His notebooks at this time reveal that he resented being regarded as one of the "castle officials," especially since his opinions about the character and purpose of the monastic life were changing rapidly.[10] He found himself rejecting both the old medieval view which had initially attracted him and the kind of modernizing that went on through the 1950s and 1960s. Overcome by feelings of instability once again, he wrote to Jacques Maritain in 1960 that he had never felt so strongly that he had "no place" in the world.[11]

He bridled at the sound of the machinery that was used for the monastery farm and wondered whether his community was not undermining its fundamental purpose. He noted sullenly that each year the tractors got bigger and louder and his reaction to machines of any kind approached revulsion. He bristled at the "insane racket" made by a passing helicopter, noting wryly that the word "chopper" was appropriate: "Insect body, thin tail, half dragonfly, half grasshopper" (p. 279). He labelled a new mechanical mower in the monastery pasture a "Behemoth," likening it to an "agricultural pagoda" (p. 279). In general he felt the machinery to be part of the incipient pragmatism that was overtaking the community that he had thought he would feel part of forever.

His situation was exacerbated by his relationship with his

abbot, a man with whom he felt profoundly out of sympathy and the man most responsible for turning Gethsemani into a modern and efficient operation. The two men were so different from each other that it was, from Merton's point of view at least, almost a textbook case of artist versus philistine. The situation was aggravated by Merton's belief that the modernizing undertaken by Dom James Fox masked an underlying reactionary spirit and that the real modernizing required in the contemplative life — changes in lifestyle, ritual, and organization — were given no attention whatsoever. In dark moments he found himself wishing that the monastic life was "less of a perpetual cold war" between subjects and superiors (p. 245).

His disaffection included the community routines and the pious clichés that seemed to him to cause the contemplative life to stagnate. He was appalled, for example, by a talk given by a visiting abbot in which it was proposed that the contemplative life consisted in clinging by force to the idea one had on entering the novitiate. Merton thought this view preposterous, and he felt increasingly alienated from a community which appeared to accept the idea with equanimity.

He reacted abrasively to the simpering manner of one of the readers in the dining hall who dropped his voice at the merest intimation of pleasure or merriment in his text, and yet who, when he came to words like "death" or "dead," laid them down "squarely" in the middle of the refectory "with satisfaction and with utter finality" (p. 11). It all seemed to Merton symptomatic of the wooden spirituality that had overtaken the community, a community now stifled by interminable "pontifical maneuverings" in ritual and strangled by "solemn, feudal, and unbreathable fictions" (p. 269). He tried to cure his case of spiritual claustrophobia temporarily by heading for one of the small lakes on the abbey's property where he would open his lungs and mind to the natural life around him. On such occasions, he wrote, the "alleluias" that had been suppressed by the stupefying weight of elaborate liturgy "came back by themselves" (p. 270).

It was clear that something had to give, and after 1963 Merton was permitted to live much of the time in a newly constructed hermitage on a wooded hill near the monastery. After 1965 he was allowed to live there fulltime with the exception that he had to be present at the community's noonday meal, a provision that was intended to protect his fragile health. As a hermit, a life that he had desired for some years, he relaxed, became more expansive in outlook, and some of the earlier lyricism returned to his journal. He decorated his hermitage with an ikon of Elias, with whom he had always identified, and he felt an excitement in its presence and in his new setting that recalls some of the more evocative scenes in *The Sign of Jonas:*

A great red globe of fiery light and glory, with angelic horses rearing up in unison inside it, drawing a simple Russian peasant's cart with the prophet standing in it, looking toward the great globe of the divine darkness to which he ascends — the blackness of the divine mystery. . . .What a thing to have in the room. It transfigures everything. (p. 270)

His eyes fondly took in all of the elements of his new hilltop vantage point, which was halfway between the night stars and the settlements below. Now that he had once again found his place in the scheme of things, he found himself warming in his feelings toward the world outside. He seemed to have outgrown the need for the warmth, protection, and certitude that had brought him into a monastic community in the first place, and he was now in a mood to engage the world not only as a Trappist monk but on his own. His revitalized contact with his fellow men was stimulated in part by his more frequent trips to Louisville, which were usually made for medical reasons. In downtown Louisville, on one occasion, he found himself "overwhelmed with the realization that I loved all those people, that they were mine and I theirs, that we could not be alien to one another even though we were total strangers." He describes his feeling as like waking from a "dream of separateness," a "spurious" illusion of being different from everybody else (p. 140).

The structure of *Conjectures of a Guilty Bystander* involves not only a movement outward, but a corresponding movement inward as well, a crisis of identity brought about by the exterior passivity of Merton's role as a comtemplative — his being what he termed a "guilty bystander." The change in his thinking was based on his fresh perception — which replaced his earlier indifference toward a world he regarded as doomed — that man's interpretation of himself was decisive in determining his destiny. Thus, the view of man that was promulgated throughout society became crucial, and Merton decided to make his own view of man as widely known as possible in the hope of altering the direction of society. He thus became a talking monk, as much of a contradiction to others, finally, as he had always been to himself. Others did not always accept the changes in him peacefully. He recoiled at the news in 1968 that some "fanatical Catholics" in Louisville, presumably infuriated by his writings on racism and on the Viet Nam war, had burned his books.[12]

He found himself drawn to the side of the social activists during the 1960s. "There is in many of them," he wrote, "a peculiar quality of truth" that conventional Christians had "rinsed out of themselves in hours of secure right-thinking and noncommitment" (p. 225). What bothered Merton was the stolid inactivity of his own Church. He wished wistfully that it was less a "Church of paper," less smothered by authority, "sitting in its office, with all the windows open, trying to hold down, with both hands, all the important papers and briefs, all the bits of red tape" (p. 228). There were exceptions — like Daniel Berrigan, the Jesuit poet and activist who, Merton wrote, "exorcised my weariness, my suspiciousness, my dark thoughts" — but such people seemed to him to be rare (p. 229).

The social radicalism in *Conjectures of a Guilty Bystander* did not entirely supplant the traditionalism of Merton's thought. His viewpoint in the journal is characterized by the tautness and balance that were always part of his most exciting writing. In the face of contemporary moral relativism, for example, he held to a belief in an "objective moral good," which brought out and confirmed the "inner significance of our life when we obey its norms" (p. 103). He thought the logical positivists absurd and sterile. He was deeply suspicious of totalitarian socialism as a remedy for the ills brought about by capitalism. He felt relieved that Christianity was around to speak to modern man's alienation and to help contemporary man overcome his suicidal "refusal of himself" (p. 293).

The distinction of *Conjectures of a Guilty Bystander* lies in the range and complexity of Merton's thought, thought whose development is delicately traced from the moment it dawns in consciousness. The growing complexity of his viewpoint led to some novel and incisive perceptions — as in his view of the subconscious. The contemplative life had stimulated an awareness of changes in himself that had worked themselves up from the subconscious, and he came to wonder about his responsibility for the contents of the dark, teeming world. He was painfully aware of how emotions from the subconscious could induce moods that were at odds with his conscious states: "I am a joyful person," he wrote in his journal, "I like life, and I have really nothing to complain of. Then suddenly a tide of this unexpected chill comes up out of the depths: and I breathe the cold air of darkness, the sense of void" (p. 239).

He felt that the abstractness of the religious life, which focused on pure intentions and interior acts, had led to both an "evasive ethic of good intentions" and, more seriously perhaps, to pathological behavior, behavior that might well be dominated by a "brutal, selfish, cruelly unjust, greedy, and murderous unconscious" (p. 98). The remedy was to bring one's "whole" house in order by the "humble acknowledgement of reality in all its depths," through psychoanalysis if necessary, a process in which he himself became involved in the 1950s. The novelty of Merton's position as a moralist was his belief that one was responsible for the contents of the subconscious, particularly for any evil that lurked there. He expressed this sense of responsibility in his own life by laying out for the reader some of the dreams that he felt were not only the creative expression of his subconscious but guides to what he should do about his moral and intellectual state.

The most interesting and elaborate dream is one in which he is invited to a party attended by elegantly attired people who promenade along the waterfront of a small fishing village. Suddenly all of the guests disappear, and Merton realizes that the party is farther away than he thought it would be. To get there he must cross a body of water. He tries to go in a boat, but it will not budge and he sees that he will have to swim: "From the clear depths of the water comes a wonderful life to which I am not entitled, a life and a power which I both love and fear. I know that by diving down into the water I can find wonders and joys, but that it is not for me to dive down; rather I must go to the other side" (p. 20). He sees a child on the opposite shore near a summer house, and he strikes out vigorously in that direction. He arrives, knowing that the child "will come, and He comes." The child's smile is that of a "Great One, hidden" and he gives the swimmer two pieces of buttered white bread, the "ritual and hieratic meal given to all who come to stay" (p. 20).

Merton used the dream as a symbol of his subconscious attachment to a way of life that he was beginning to have doubts about on the conscious level. The symbolism of the water is especially intriguing, representing a sensuous state of restful exploration — nature, death, the womb, an imaginative fall into the sexual release enjoyed by other men. The dream points to a destiny that he believed to be more essential, profound, and exhausting than that held out by his community — an active and solitary quest of God. Hence the tension that lies at the heart of *Conjectures of a Guilty Bystander*.

The tension expresses itself in the style of Merton's descriptions of things. The descriptions are as vivid as ever, but far more tentative and shifting than in the earlier journals:

> Beauty of sunlight falling on a tall vase of red and white carnations and green leaves on the altar of the novitiate chapel. The light and dark. The darkness of the fresh, crinkled flower; light, warm and red, all around the darkness. The flower is the same color as blood, but it is in no sense whatever "as red as blood." Not at all! It is as red as a carnation. Only that. (p. 131)

Shimmering with beauty, the flowers will not be steadied, and in the excitement of Merton's perception, they serve as a temporary medium for the passage of God: "He passes. He remains. We pass. In and out. He passes. We remain. We are nothing. We are everything. He is in us. He is gone from us. He is not here. We are here in Him." At this point he questions the moment of epiphany as a possible illusion. "But no matter," he continues, "for illusion is the shadow of reality and reality is the grace and gift that underlies all these lights, these colors, this silence" (p. 131). The shuttling of his mind and imagination back and forth in this way is typical of *Conjectures of a Guilty Bystander* and is one of the centers of drama in the book.

The final settling of Merton's perceptions on the literal reality of the vase of flowers, rather than on their importance as foci of the divine presence, symbolized his entrance into a Zen-like world in which things are what they are and in which their very existence is sufficient to give them radiance. Part of this attitude involved an acceptance of the limits of his poetic rearranging of experience: "Dark dawn. Streaks of pale red, under a few high clouds. A pattern of clothes lines, clothes pins, shadowy saplings. Abstraction. There is no way to capture it. Let it be" (p. 227). The imagination could get carried away—moving by analogy from cloud to clothes line to tree, until finally the concreteness and immediacy of the scene had been lost. Nevertheless, he clung to nature more ardently than ever in this time of uncertainty, delighting in the sunrise with its "enormous yolk of energy" and in the sounds of the waking birds (p. 268). Paradise, he reflected, was all around us. There was nothing conjectural, he decided, about that.

Between *Conjectures of a Guilty Bystander* and the *Asian Journal*, Merton published "Day of a Stranger" (1967). The piece begins with his becoming aware of a jet flying over his hermitage—"out of my world"—carrying passengers in their "isolated, arbitrary lounge" to some distant city. The occasion serves as the basis of a series of reflections structured around the cycle of the day. These reflections are organized into two main motifs—that of seasonal time as symbolized by the woods and birds, and that of clock time that is symbolized by the jet, by the SAC bombers that the jet brings to mind, and by modern technocracy in general.

Merton does not picture himself as a stranger because of his physical isolation, since he indicates that those thrown randomly together in the jet are also strangers to one another. He at least knew and was known by the creatures in his immediate surroundings: "I know the birds in fact very well, for there are precise pairs of birds (two each of fifteen) living in the immediate area of my cabin." He portrays himself as forming a balance with the woods and animals—he supplying the consciousness while they supply the energy and grace. His participation in the wooded scene gives his surroundings a "new configuration" and a new harmony.[13]

He was to give the world a sense of what it meant to be awake and aware of the universe at night and until the dawn: "I find myself in the primordial lostness of night, solitude, forest, peace, a mind awake in the dark, looking for a light, not totally reconciled to being out of bed."[14] "The sweet dark warmth of the whole world would have to be my wife," he reflected. He could be useful in drawing out the meaning of the darkness and the silence, which symbolized the "virginal point of pure nothingness which is at the center of all other loves."[15] In this sense all men were strangers, and, just as their love arose from the void, so too did the new day whose dawn he felt it necessary to witness in the name of all humanity.

Before leaving on his Asian journey in 1968, Merton kept a journal of his trips to California, New Mexico, and Alaska. He called the journal "Woods, Shore, Desert." The manuscript throws light on his state of mind preparatory to his climactic journey. He was overwhelmed by the northern California coastline and thought of setting up his hermitage there. His imagination caught fire at the sight of the Pacific surf: "Low tide. Long rollers trail white sleeves of foam behind them, reaching for the sand, like hands for the keyboard of an instrument."[16]

Part of the spell was due to the fact that it was the Asian ocean, and his thoughts were very much on the momentous journey that lay before him. Immersed in Zen at this point, he forced his perceptions to slow, to give each one time to "settle in the heart."[17] The giant redwoods were too much for him, however, and back in Kentucky, he could not sleep at night for thinking about them: "Who can see such trees," he wondered, "and bear to be away from them?"[18]

The *Asian Journal* was published posthumously in 1973. It is obviously rougher than it would have been had Merton had a chance to edit it. The journal covers his visits to various parts of Asia in the fall of 1968, his attendance at ecumenical conferences in Calcutta and Bangkok, meetings with Hindu and Buddhist scholars, and trips to the mountains of Ceylon and to the Himalayas, where he met with the Dalai Lama. The book is a potpourri of observations, meditations, travel notes, poetic fragments, all set down in an accelerated style that is almost vertiginous at times. The atmosphere of the *Asian Journal* is intensely nomadic. The speed of many of the entries shows Merton's imagination racing, notably in the "Kandy Express," which echoes the rhythm of a bizarre train ride.

The itinerant atmosphere of the *Asian Journal* is heightened by Merton's sense that the length of his stay was "indeterminate."[19] His friend Edward Rice recalls that his strongest impression at the time was that Merton did not intend to return to Gethsemani.[20] Although he regarded his final destination as an "open question," however, Merton found himself appreciating his Kentucky hermitage more than he had "last summer when things seemed so noisy and crowded."[21] The possibilities seemed endless. He considered, for example, giving part of his time to the setting up of a Tibetan meditation center in America, probably in the New Mexican desert. He considered placing himself, temporarily at least, in one of the loosely-knit groups of Tibetan contemplatives under the direction of a guru. The problem, he thought to himself, was finding the man, since he was "not exactly dizzy with the idea of looking for a magic master" (p. 82). He felt that the Buddhists were the most promising practitioners of the contemplative life in the world, and there were moments when he was strongly tempted to fade into the Asian landscape: "When we went on up the mountain from Swarg Ashram I heard a great commotion in the tall trees and looked up to see marvelous gray apes with black faces crashing and swinging through the branches. They were huge, almost as big as people. . . . It would be wonderful to live in a hermitage with apes in the trees around it" (p. 96).

In spite of the accelerated pace of the *Asian Journal* the tone is the most detached of all the journals. The detachment is apparent in the scenes in which Merton pondered the social misery that was so conspicuous and abundant throughout Asia. Calcutta is viewed as having "the lucidity of despair, of absolute confusion, of vitality helpless to cope with itself" in which what each person wanted inevitably led to the "denial of the desires of all the others" (p. 28). The descriptions of Calcutta are among the most stirring and memorable in the *Asian Journal*, but they are reserved in tone, lacking the reformist zeal that he had manifested in *Conjectures of a Guilty Bystander:*

> The vast noise of Calcutta seems somehow to be also a silence. There was a spectacular robbery on Sudder Street three weeks ago and it is a city of crime; somehow the crime gets lost in the sheer massive poverty and exhaustion — the innocence of despair. For the masses of Calcutta, you dimly begin to think, there is no judgment. Only their misery. And instead of being judged, they are a judgment on the rest of the world. Yet curiously non-prophetic . . . nonaccusatory. Passive. Not exactly resentful. Not yet. . . . One imagines an enormous, elemental, thoughtless, confused violence like that of a sweeping storm of rain after a sultry summer day. Will it cleanse anything? Clear the air? Will the city simply go on stifling in its own steam? It breathes, sprawls, broods, sweats, moves, lies down, and gets up again. (p. 132)

Merton foresaw a coming social revolution as well as the causes that would propel it, but he appears somewhat removed and skeptical about the final effects of the impending upheaval. His language is temperate and his point of view philosophical. The aesthetic qualities of the scene appear to have meant as much to him as the injustice and misery embedded in his unhappy subject. It was not that he lacked sympathy, but rather that his perspective had enlarged significantly.

In this light it is not surprising to discover that the principal theme of the *Asian Journal* is consciousness. Put flatly this way, the journal might appear duller than it is. However, the energy of the journal derives from its portrayal of the shaping of consciousness in a man who is caught up passionately in a quest for transcendental vision. What makes the book dramatically interesting is Merton's determination not to be faked. The combination of tough-mindedness and the idealistic quest for sublime awareness is what gives the *Asian Journal* its particular appeal.

Having been immersed in the study of consciousness through his interest in Zen, he felt the power of his own consciousness awakened by the things he saw in Asia. One of the most enticing of these experiences was his view of the Himalayan peak, Kanchenjunga: "There is another side of Kanchenjunga and of every mountain," he wrote — "the side that has never been photographed and turned into post cards." That was the only side, he concluded, "worth seeing" (p. 153). In his desire to think of Asia as offering examples of permanence, he caught himself resenting the snowslides of Kanchenjunga and preferring the "postcard" mountain to the real one (p. 150). Thus forewarned, he determined to avoid illusions.

Such illusions, he estimated, would most likely occur when his sensibility was aroused by beauty and his mind hungry for meaning. On a tea plantation in the mountains of Ceylon, for example, he looked back critically at his experience in India and decided that there had been too much "'looking for' something: an answer, a vision, 'something other,' And this breeds illusion. Illusion that there *is* something else." It all led, he felt, to the old "splitting-up process," by which he presumably meant ratiocination, which he now thought of as "mindlessness" compared to the Zen-like "mindfulness" of seeing "all-in-emptiness and not having to break it up against itself" (p. 148).

In spite of his caution he valued Asia's ability to give him fresh perspectives, as in a night walk along the shore in Ceylon: "A hot night. Warm, rubbery waves shining under the moon . . . A new strange feeling out there — westward nothing until Africa. And out there—to the south, nothing till Antarctica . . . I was shocked to see Orion hanging almost upside down in the north" (p. 214). Even the seductive Mount Kanchenjunga could be made finally to yield perceptions that one might trust. In spite of the shifting pantomime of the mountain's appearance with the changing of the light — white spiraling snow and cloud in the daytime and a few "discreet showings of whorehouse pink" in the evening — the full beauty of the mountain could be appreciated under certain conditions. The observer had to accept the fact that what he experienced contained a subjective reality in addition to an objective one. On rare occasions, though, when the mind settled into a quiet attentiveness, " the smoke of ideas" cleared and the mountain was seen (pp. 156-157).

Because he was resolved to be skeptical, the breakthrough in consciousness which Merton achieved at Polonnaruwa in Ceylon hit him with as much surprise as exhilaration. The huge stone Buddhas, one seated and the other reclining, both symbolized and made possible the sort of sublime relationship with the world around him that his studies of Eastern religions had been preparing him for. The quiet smiles of the Buddhas were filled with "every possibility, questioning nothing, knowing everything, rejecting nothing, the peace not of emotional resignation but of Madhyamika, of sunyata, that has seen through every question without trying to discredit anyone or anything — *without refutation*" (p. 233).

He marvelled at the pattern of the scene, the "clarity and fluidity of shape and line, the design of the monumental bodies composed into the rock shape and landscape, figure, rock and tree" (p. 233). Aware of his tendency to transmute his aesthetic responses into mystical intuitions, he spelled out the exact nature of the experience: "I don't know when in my life I have ever had such a sense of beauty and spiritual validity running together in one aesthetic illumination" (p. 235). The illumination at Polonnaruwa clearly represents the point of arrival in a book whose structure is that of a pilgrimage. Polonnaruwa symbolized Asia "in its purity," all that Merton felt he had been "obscurely" looking for. He had "pierced" the surface, passing beyond the "shadow and the disguise" (p. 236). Having thus scaled the heights of consciousness, his accidental death shortly afterwards takes on an almost choreographed quality.

Although the *Asian Journal* is limited by the arbitrary setting out of its subjects and by the wide diversity in the relative importance of these subjects, nevertheless the book succeeds by virtue of the character of its narrator. As a literary form, the diary is singularly illustrative of the rule that what is important in writing is not the majesty of the subject but the sensibility of the teller, and in this respect the reader of Merton's diaries is richly rewarded. For all of the *Asian Journal's* fine descriptive shades and stirring themes, the book's interest lies finally not only in what Merton makes of the world around him but in what he makes of his own variegated consciousness glimpsed in the midst of these explorations. The journal shimmers with self-consciousness, held at a high pitch and then walked around as an object of interest in itself.

Although the diaries represent the least conspicuous examples of Merton's art, they are very possibly the richest and the most memorable. He had always thought he would be remembered for his poetry, but as was the case with Thoreau, whom he so much admired, it is the journals that stick in the mind. Moreover, it is in the journals that the particular contribution that Merton made to twentieth century literature can be most easily distinguished. It is there that he spoke most poignantly about the gnawing alienation that he felt burdened modern man, an alienation that he helped to overcome in others as he had overcome it in himself — by making himself naked before the gaze of all.

Notes

[1]"First and Last Thoughts," in *A Thomas Merton Reader*, ed. Thomas P. McDonnell (New York, 1962), p. vii.
[2]*A Hidden Wholeness: The Visual World of Thomas Merton* (Boston, 1970), p. 9.
[3]*The Secular Journal of Thomas Merton* (New York, 1959), p. viii.
[4]Paul Elmen, "Already in Custody," *Christian Century*, LXXXVI (1959), p. 1215.
[5]*Secular Journal*, p. 147. Subsequent references will be incorporated in the text.
[6]*The Sign of Jonas* (New York, 1953), p. 11. Subsequent references will be incorporated in the text.
[7]Mark Van Doren, *Autobiography* (New York, 1958), p. 330.
[8]"The True Legendary Sound: The Poetry and Criticism of Edwin Muir," *Sewanee Review*, LXXV (1967), p. 318.
[9]*Conjectures of a Guilty Bystander* (New York, 1966), p. 224. Subsequent references will be incorporated in the text.
[10]Notebook #85 (1967).
[11]Letter to Jacques Maritain, Feb. 22, 1960.
[12]Letter to Ernesto Cardenal, March 15, 1968.
[13]"Day of a Stranger," *Hudson Review*, XX (1967), p. 212. Subsequent references will be incorporated in the text.

[14]Ibid., p. 214.
[15]Ibid., p. 211.
[16]"Woods, Shore, Desert," p. 13. Manuscript.
[17]Ibid., p. 14.
[18]Ibid., p. 41.
[19]"Circular Letter to Friends," September, 1968. Mimeograph.
[20]*Man in the Sycamore Tree*, p. 124.
[21]*The Asian Journal of Thomas Merton*, ed. Naomi Burton, Br. Patrick Hart, James Laughlin, and Amiya Chakravarty (New York, 1973), p. 103. Subsequent references will be incorporated in the text.

Essayist

MERTON PUBLISHED OVER 250 essays and over 20 expository books, many of which were collections of his essays. He worked best within the short frame of the essay. The titles of the collections were usually broad enough to serve as an umbrella for diverse essays. He would often overlook the fact that some of the essays were repetitive, and it was characteristic of him to compose a number of essays in which similar themes and images were used. Parts of *Prometheus: A Meditation* (1958), for example, show up in *The Behaviour of Titans* (1961) and also appear unheralded in *The New Man* (1961). A paragraph from the brief preface to *Silence in Heaven* (1956) appears in the later volume *Seasons of Celebration* (1964).

Merton's reusing of old material resulted from the large number of requests for him to supply essays, a demand that seemed to him to have become insatiable by the late 1960s. Moreover, he liked to place his ideas in different contexts in order to bring out a nuance that had been latent in other settings. Repetition was in fact a ritualistic aspect of his method of developing his thought. In this connection, in *My Argument with the Gestapo* the narrator argues that it is necessary to "go back and start from the beginning and make over all the definitions for ourselves again."[1] In "First and Last Thoughts" Merton contended that no one need have a compulsion to be original in everything he wrote and that a writer often developed by saying the "same thing again" on a "deeper level." In this way the old was "recovered on a new plane" and thereby became a "new reality."[2]

Consequently, Merton's style often involves circling over a subject, repeating and revising his ideas until they are firmly planted in the reader's mind and only then going on to the next stage of the discussion. The method not only emphasized lucidity, but was his way of groping toward the ramifications of his seminal ideas. Fortunately, because of the gracefulness and fluency of his prose style, the reader is often unaware of the repetition. The following excerpt from his introduction to a book by Ernesto Cardenal will illustrate the point: "For every love that is not a totally free and spontaneous self-giving, harbors a taste of death. This means that all our love — the love of us average human beings, who are neither saints nor mystics—is beset with contradiction, conflict and bitterness. And it carries with it a taste of death."[3] Circular — and yet, because of its suppleness and rhythm — softly persuasive.

The gnawing question about Merton as essayist is : how did he as a cloistered monk get the information that formed the basis for such a prolific output? He read voraciously and eclectically, and he made notes on everything. His notebooks contain excerpts from his reading on the right-hand pages and his reactions to these notes on the left. He read in nearly every area of knowledge except the physical sciences. He received books and magazines from friends when these were not available in the monastery's rather good library, and he was especially interested in receiving liberal periodicals like the *Nation* and *I. F. Stone's Weekly*.

He used his royalty account to order new books for himself, and picked up a lot of information from his many correspondents and visitors. The flow of information into him became more and more reliable as the monastery's system of censorship relaxed in the 1960s. In addition, he wrote to his publisher, James Laughlin, that on his trips to town he would usually drop in at the University of Louisville in order to catch up with what was going on.[4] As well, he met with artists and intellectuals in order to keep abreast of what was going on in the arts in his own area. He wrote to his friend W. H. Ferry in 1961 that he often had guests at the abbey, and he continued this practice when he moved into the hermitage.[5]

He complained to Ferry later on, however, that he frequently had to depend on late, "second hand news"[6] and he wrote to another friend that he was "not properly informed," since his knowledge was sometimes dependent on magazines that he had leafed through in doctors' offices.[7] He conceded in another letter that some of his "sweeping judgments" were not based on a "full battery of facts" and that what he dealt with most of all were "impressions."[8] At other times he came to value his remoteness. If it was true that news had become stale by the time it reached him, the delay could be seen as an advantage. Through this delayed perspective, he felt that he was better able to distinguish the "real happening" from the "pseudo-event," a useful capacity, he concluded, when one considered that nine-tenths of what was carried in the media consisted of manufactured events.[9]

He did not hesitate to borrow ideas from others, and in fact the bulk of his essays is principally composed of such borrowings. He was primarily a reactor to the ideas of others, although his reactions frequently led to some original observations. He was in the habit of asking not about details, but about the direction in which events were moving. He described his essay style as "simply thinking out loud"[10] and pictured himself as a "solitary explorer."[11] A number of critics have made the point that he was not a systematic thinker. Although he set forth lucidly and vigorously a number of important themes, he usually did so in a fragmentary, tentative manner. He regarded himself as an intuitive rather than a systematic writer. He might more aptly be described, though, as a rational man who had a deep distrust of rationality.

The tone of Merton's essays is one of the most appealing aspects of his writing. His approach is conversational, personal, and exploratory, the voice of a man who wants to join with the reader in order to clarify a particular question. Although he frequently draws on his own experience, he tends not to place himself in the foreground, and gives the impression of a man totally absorbed by his subject. His manner is urbane and tactful, and although he was capable of bombast, he tried to be restrained and ironic when he felt himself in a reformist mood. He explained the reason for this restraint in a letter to a friend in 1964: "If at all possible, one should try to say things in such a way as not to be dismissed out of hand as a man spoiling for a fight and a born trouble maker. I know one cannot say anything valid without getting this reputation. Yet I always hope that things can be said in such a way that even the stuffiest people may have no excuse for not hearing it."[12]

If Merton strove for a tone that was flexible and conciliatory, his vantage point was not: it was apocalyptic. He was convinced that modern man was likely to carry out point by point the "harlotries" of the Apocalypse, even if justified and sublimated through some "clean sociological explanation."[13] He wrote in his notebook in 1967 that the time seemed right for the coming of the apocalyptic beast, a time when man was "completely self-assured."[14] He portrayed the contemporary period as a "time of no room," which was simultaneously the "time of the end," a time when everyone was obsessed with "lack of time, lack of space, with saving time, conquering space" — only to project into time and space the "anguish produced within them by the technological furies of size, volume, quantity, speed, number, price, power and acceleration."[15] The stiffening effect of Merton's apocalyptic perspective was mitigated by the exploratory movement of his mind. The tentativeness of his approach was linked to his conviction that one "can't have faith without doubt" and his consequent resolution not to suppress doubt.[16] If his eschatological vision gave his writing power, his tentativeness kept that writing from becoming doctrinaire.

Merton characteristically begins his essays with an anecdote or a tableau that epitomizes his theme. He begins an essay on Gandhi, for example, with a vivid account of the meeting in London between Gandhi and some British statesmen over the question of British rule in India. He portrays Gandhi as emerging from the fog and slums of London in light tropical clothing and attracting the puzzled and patronizing stares of Englishmen at his gauntness, his bald head, and his naked brown legs. The figure of Gandhi is quickly used to illustrate the people whose cause he represented, a cause that was in conflict with the interests of a mystified and obstinate Western power. Gandhi is "Asia, wise, disconcerting, in many ways unlovely, but determined upon some inscrutable project and probably very holy."[17]

Merton's weakness as a visual writer is his fondness for sensational illustration and his attraction to stereotypes. In *Seeds of Destruction* (1964), for example, he showed a tendency to pin his convictions to single, sometimes lurid examples — like the white Eagle scout "who had been to Sunday School *and* to a racist rally," and who then went out and killed a black boy. Similarly, there is the Louisiana priest who, because he allowed white and black children to receive communion at the same time, "though at different ends of the altar rail," was beaten by some of his parishioners.[18] It was because of such illustrating that Merton sometimes oversimplified. He was best when he trusted to his own impressions and sensibility, weakest when he relied on journalistic fodder.

He usually structured his essays dialectically, placing two ideas in symmetrical opposition to each other. He hoped by this device to find the "unity and clarity" that he believed emerged from tension and paradox.[19] Characteristically, the clash of opposites in his writing resulted in a helix-shaped ascent to the level of illumination that he sought. In his essay on "Mount Athos," for example, he juxtaposes the religiously symbolic bonfires of the ancient and remote Greek monastery with the atomic light of the "mushroom-like pillar of death," working the two kinds of light into each other until the reader's vision of the contemporary world is transformed.[20]

Merton's essays are frequently syntheses of historical facts and myths that he grafted onto contemporary experience. This method involved him not only in dialectics but also in the discovery of significant analogies. Possessed of a very retentive memory, he had a mind rich in associations. People and ideas, ancient and modern, were constantly brushing in his consciousness, and he was frequently struck with some of the resemblances that turned up. An early anchorite, for example, seemed to him to be a kind of "sixth-century desert Hemingway."[21] Both Marx and Freud reminded him of various orthodox spiritual writers, and he showed how an ancient Confucian text anticipated some of Freud's insights by twenty centuries "in all simplicity and without benefit of the Oedipus complex."[22] He characterized the fathers of the Church as possessed of "psychological finesse" for their psychoanalysis of the relationship between pride, anxiety, and compulsiveness. He threw together bizarre combinations in his essays, creating a sort of intellectual casserole that included contemporary anthropologists, Zen mystics, Taoist philosophers, European existentialists, and Nazi war criminals.[23] The range was staggering. His method, he believed, was simple: "What we have to do is to discover what is useful to us. We can then discard structures that don't help. And if it turns out that something medieval helps, keep it."[24]

A good example of Merton's synthesizing is his essay "Rain and the Rhinoceros," which was collected in *Raids on the Un-*

speakable (1966). Set against the background of a rainy evening, the essay brings together the figures of Thoreau, Ionesco, and the ancient Syrian thinker, Philoxenos. Skillfully, Merton leads the reader as if by a random sequence of associations from the sound of the rain to the recollection of Thoreau's isolation with nature and finally to a study of the collective versus the individual consciousness, using Ionesco's play *Rhinoceros* as the focus for the discussion. The essay combines narrative elements with lucid intellectual synthesis.

The basis of Merton's synthesizing was his desire to unite within himself the discrete truths that he had recognized in others. He regarded his effort as an attunement to all of the "syllables of the great song," believing that violence and destructiveness came from the fact that "we cling madly to a single syllable."[25] He told a friend in 1961 that he saw his task as one of a "very remote preparation" for future generations by synthesizing within himself all that was "best and most true in the various great spiritual traditions."[26] In spite of his isolation he took pains constantly to emphasize the analogy between his situation and that of other men. He wrote to a correspondent in 1966, for example, that although he had not "sweated out twenty-five years of marital fidelity," he had had twenty-five years in the monastery without leaving and it was "much the same kind of a problem."[27]

He received even greater impetus from his feeling that his Church had not always remained faithful to its mission to unify the world. Christianity, he felt, had made its way in the world of the first century "not by imposing Jewish cultural and social standards on the rest of the world, but by abandoning them, getting free of them so as to be 'all things to all men.'"[28] Unhappily, he concluded, that openness in approaching the world had been abandoned by the end of the Middle Ages. He looked toward a state of "final integration" within the world and within individual consciousnesses, a "deeper, fuller identity" than that which was contained in the limited "ego-self" that he regarded as a "fragment" of a man's being.[29] As was often the case with Merton, his style of synthesizing grew out of the configuration of his own life. The style was the man.

In spite of Merton's espousal of unity, the *persona* in his essays is paradoxically that of the outsider. He did not project himself as an outsider because of an antipathy to the idea of community, but rather because he had evolved out of the community. The contemplative's chief duty, finally, was his own development. Merton perceived the monk, therefore, as not simply living on the margin of the world, but as creating a lifestyle that surpassed those lived in the world. The monk who became an outsider from, and yet on behalf of, his society was like a tulip, Merton told a friend: Tulips were not "important," they were "essential."[30] The monk was given freedom and independence — if he chose to recognize these — by the very absurdity of his way of life: "Man without woman," he felt, is absurd.[31] The monk's freakishness and loneliness, although a kind of death, could illustrate in a conspicuous way the void of loneliness locked within others and thus encourage a sensitivity to the human condition.

The monk as outsider could be a symbol of freedom to those in the larger society who felt defeated. Merton stressed repeatedly that the monk's role as solitary placed him outside social institutions and conventionalism. His function was both to protest against the shallowness and perfidy of the established order and to awaken the dormant interior lives of other men. He tried to fulfill this function in his own case by striving to perfect his interior life and by revealing his struggle to others.

The solitude that he pursued in so open a manner was the same solitude that he believed all men felt. While it made some men vulnerable by causing them to feel lonely, it also gave them the insight and energy to avoid group thinking. Merton likened the monk to social radicals, and he noted with some chagrin that these people had taken over the function once performed by the monk.[32] He disliked the tendency of some people, including religiously oriented people, to make themselves, in a chameleon-like manner, relevant to their times. Nevertheless, he believed that the monk should recognize that even if he had detached himself from some of the corruptive forces in society, he was still immersed in history and responsible for it. In this connection he especially admired figures — like the eighteenth century vagrant saint, Benedict Labre — who slipped hidden through their times only to explode in society's consciousness once the meaning of their apparently futile lives surfaced.

The outsider's natural setting was the desert, a recurrent symbol in Merton's writing. A descendant of the ancient desert fathers, the contemplative could end up living literally in the desert as some of Merton's fellow Trappists did in New Mexico. If not actually living in a desert setting, however, the monk was at least destined to lead a wilderness existence. The contemplative thus entered a blank world that was valuable to him precisely because it had no value to anyone else. The desert world of the solitary was, Merton warned, the "country of madness" and the "home of despair."[33] It was not a place for the weak. Thrown back introspectively upon himself, the solitary clings to his sanity as a drowning man clings to a straw, feeling always on the edge of a spiritual "cataclysm" and always searching for landmarks in his "trackless" wilderness.[34] The ordeal involved surviving an arid and isolated existence without drying up inside: "For if emotions really die in the desert," Merton wrote, "our humanity dies with them."[35] If he pulled through, the solitary could become everyman, visibly taking on his shoulders the solitude and the essential poverty of all men.

It has been observed that there is no earlier or later Merton because, as Frederick Joseph Kelly has put it, he "never repudiated the fundamental ideas of his past."[36] While it is true that Merton held to certain ideas throughout his life, he experienced a major change in outlook during the 1960s and came to regret some of the ideas that he had emphasized in earlier writings. In the evaluation of his own work that he did in the late 1960s, he downgraded much of the earlier expository writing. In retrospect he saw himself in the early period as a "superficially pious, rather rigid and somewhat narrow-minded young monk."[37]

He felt more comfortable with the writing that was more personal, literary, and contemplative. One of the things that he disliked in the early writing was its pronounced asceticism, which seemed at times to have been postulated as an end in itself. A brief example from *The Ascent to Truth* (1951) will suffice: "The earthly desires men cherish are shadows. There is no true happiness in fulfilling them. Why, then, do we continue to pursue joys without substance? Because *the pursuit itself* has become our only substitute for joy. Unable to rest in anything we achieve, we determine to forget our discontent in a ceaseless quest for new satisfactions."[38] It could be argued that Merton never forsook the thoughts contained here, but it is also true that increasingly in the late 1950s he began to emphasize other things.

He came to regret the pious rhetoric of some of the early work, which was often burdened with theological and philosophical jargon. Nevertheless, his prose style was engaging and attracted a good many readers. The imagery from these early prose writings is restrained and conventional, and is accompanied by a pleasing pedagogical manner. The following is a respectable example from *Seeds of Contemplation* (1949): "As a magnifying glass concentrates the rays of the sun into a little burning knot of heat that can set fire to a dry leaf or a piece of paper, so the mysteries of Christ in the Gospel concentrate the rays of God's light and fire to a point that sets fire to the spirit of man."[39]

In 1962 Merton announced that he had done with pious pronouncements and that he would no longer limit himself to being a "spiritual" writer.[40] In addition to his taking up new themes, however, his style even as a spiritual writer changed perceptibly. This change can be seen in comparing the first version of *Seeds of Contemplation* (1949) with the *New Seeds of Contemplation* that came out in 1961. Writing in the *New Republic*, a reviewer of the first edition of the book wrote in 1949 that except for a single reference to Marxist socialism and another to the atomic bomb the reflections might have been those of a "monk of the Middle Ages."[41]

Apart from the shared metaphor of "seeds," the two versions of *Seeds of Contemplation* differ significantly. The details Merton omitted from the revised version are as noteworthy as those he retained and added. Left out of the revised edition were the passages that set forth a narrow asceticism, such as the following: "Nothing that we know and nothing that we can enjoy and desire with our natural faculties can be anything but an obstacle to the pure possession of Him as He is in Himself and therefore if we can still be satisfied with any of these things we will remain infinitely far away from Him. That is why we must be detached and delivered from them all in order to come to Him" (p. 130). He warned against the damaging influence of cities in the original version of *Seeds of Contemplation* — small consolation for the majority of people who had to live in them — but he added an important codicil in *New Seeds of Contemplation*. He observed that one could accept even the accelerated life of the city as a "seed of solitude" and urged a "sense of compassion" for those who had been so traumatized by the city that they had forgotten the "very concept of solitude."[42] In the first version Merton exhorted his readers to develop a habit of contemplation "in which your nature and your emotions and your own selfhood no longer have any part" (p. 164). In *New Seeds of Contemplation* he reversed himself, arguing that passion and emotion certainly had their place in the life of prayer.

On a stylistic level he dropped many of the earlier pious clichés and faded theological jargon. He also abandoned his rather mechanical descriptions of how to contemplate. The tone of *New Seeds of Contemplation* is more searching than that of the earlier version. To *New Seeds of Contemplation* he added the comment that: "You cannot be a man of faith unless you know how to doubt" (p. 105). In addition, he found himself wanting to qualify the solitude that he had prescribed in the original *Seeds of Contemplation*. Rather than fleeing to the mountains or desert the contemplative was urged to address himself to the realities of contemporary life and the "great formless sea of responsibility which is the crowd" (p. 54).

A mood of affirmation pervades the *New Seeds of Contemplation* which was not present in the original version. This is nowhere more visible than in the triumphant coda of the book "The Dance of Life." Seeing migrating birds descend on a grove of junipers, one catches a glimpse, Merton writes, of the cosmic dance:

> For the world and time are the dance of the Lord in emptiness. The silence of the spheres is the music of a wedding feast. The more we persist in misunderstanding the phenomena of life, the more we analyze them out into strange finalities and complex purposes of our own, the more we involve ourselves in sadness, absurdity and

despair. But it does not matter much, because no despair of ours can alter the reality of things, or stain the joy of the cosmic dance which is always there. Indeed, we are in the midst of it, and it is in the midst of us, for it beats in our very blood, whether we want it to or not. (pp. 296-297)

The passage is a lyrical manifestation of the intellectual and spiritual molting through which the earlier narrowness had been shed.

Merton's later essays tend to revolve around pivotal themes mostly concerned with society. He was disturbed by the fact that with the decline of religion and the onrush of science man's will to believe had been directed toward the state. Who, he wondered, was to judge the state? He worried about the brutalizing effect of the collective consciousness and saw that many fellow intellectuals lacked the power or the will to take on the state, or were in fact creatures of the state themselves. Hence his key notion of the innocent bystander. The intellectuals, he felt, should be like the child in "The Emperor's New Clothes," bold enough to speak out and yet innocent enough to perceive the "fault of the others."[43] Not to act was to become a "guilty" bystander.

Merton thought of individualism as the basic force in American society and the force most responsible for the social "atomism" that had led to "inertia, passivism and spiritual decay."[44] He contended that individualism fitted beautifully into the technologists' plans, giving rise to a homogeneous, acquisitive population that consumed the products of mass manufacturing. In the face of this climate of "all-embracing conformities," individuals inevitably put on a "mask of resigned and monotonous sameness," as he phrased it in *Seasons of Celebration* (1964).[45] The result, he added, was a desperate situation in which people exaggerated trivial differences between themselves as they became more and more aware of the tedium of their lives.

The binary nature of Merton's essay style is manifested in his balancing of the aggressiveness of the *individual* against the shyness and depth of the *person*—the man within. He thought of the inner self as that self that would not posture and that could not be fooled, a self that resembled a shy wild animal that rarely appeared and then only against a background of tranquillity and solitude. The growth of the person within every man was the key not only to his happiness, but to the cohesiveness of the whole society and thus had a critical bearing on the destiny of all. The depths of the inner man were limitless, mysterious, and ultimately hopeful. Merton insisted on the significance of the buried life in every man.

Technology is an obsessive theme in Merton's writing. He viewed technology as the greatest threat to the climate of silence that the interior self required in order to overcome its shyness and emerge. While recognizing that technology was clearly here to stay, he lamented its debilitating effect on people — the "deadening of spirit and of sensibility," the "blunting of perception," the "proneness to unrest and guilt."[46] He was attacked for his ingenuousness regarding technology on a number of occasions. The following is a typical example: "When Merton hears the huge machines that clatter away to shatter the natural beauty of the Kentucky countryside, he is not thinking of how they reduce back-breaking labor and add to the ease of life."[47] Merton's answer to this sort of criticism was that whatever the obvious benefits of technology were, and he freely conceded these, contemporary man had nonetheless become the captive of his scientific virtuosity.

Merton portrayed violence as issuing inevitably from modern technocracy. The two types that he focused on were racism and war. Racism was a clear example of the divisiveness and alienation that he felt were inevitable in a loveless technocracy. Similarly, he saw modern warfare as the direct result of man's passion for technology. It would be the sane administrators of modern technocracy, he believed, who would "without qualms and without nausea" aim the missiles and press the buttons that would initiate the final destruction.[48]

Competing ideologies and social systems often seemed to be the root of war, but these, Merton believed, were often merely fictions that obscured any sense of the value of the enemy as well as any perception of the similarities shared by various social systems. Caught paranoically in a web of political rhetoric in which he could no longer see things clearly, modern man resorted with relief to the concreteness of war, a "sure" means of communication, as he put it in a letter to W. H. Ferry in 1967.[49] He became disenchanted with the classical ethic of the just war which permitted an "innocent" society to defend itself. For one thing he felt that the dangers of nuclear war to the whole planet outweighed the question of moral justification. He went over the question at length in *Seeds of Destruction,* and although he did not deal convincingly with the question of how one should respond to an attack from a despot like Hitler, he tried to show some of the consequences of meeting violence with violence. For Merton, a violent reaction simply sustained the general cycle of violence that was gradually consuming the world in apocalyptic convulsions. He described the desire to kill, even in a spirit of self-defense, as like the desire to attack another person with an "ingot of red hot iron: I have to pick up the incandescent metal and burn my own hand while burning the other."[50]

The only genuine liberation from oppression, he believed, was that which freed the oppressor as well as the oppressed, and the way to do this was through nonviolent resistance to evil. He distinguished between nonviolent resistance and passivity. Nonviolence sought change, even revolution, and did everything short of being violent to bring this change about. The nonviolent resister fought not only for a particular cause or social system but for the truth in general, the enemy's truth as well as his own.

The reconstruction of the world depended, Merton believed, on its ability to turn cities into communities — two dialectical motifs that circulate through his essays. He wondered doubtfully how man would organize his life in the years to come, and he feared that the future would be an "electronic labyrinth" in which men would "hunt heads among the aerials and fire-escapes."[51] He observed that accelerated technological progress had been paralleled by regressiveness and passivity in the citizenry.

As the hub of modern technocracy, the city with its faceless slums and misery seemed to Merton to be the place where the mythology of power and war germinated. The city had supplanted the healthy communality of village life with anonymity and congestion. Isolated within his hermitage, he was nevertheless disturbed by the din of the city and the "hum of power that eats up the night."[52]

If it was important for the modern city to recover a sense of community and identity, that recovery seemed unlikely. The only way, Merton came to believe, was through the study of the successful cities of ancient peoples, some of whom lingered in a relatively primitive state in the contemporary world. It was this search that underlay his strong interest in anthropology throughout the 1960s. Through his studies of the Mayans, for example, he concluded that the first cities on the North American continent were "centers for celebration," lacking armies and kings and oriented toward the ritual celebration of nature, the community, and the cosmos.[53] He regarded some of the indigenous cultures of North America as rooted in a past that had never been surpassed. He regretted that the European missionaries had not recognized the cultural wealth of the indigenous peoples of the new world, thereby impoverishing their own subsequent history as well as that of those whom they conquered and proselytized.

The richness of early American cities derived from the particular mythdream that lay at the base of their culture. He described the mythdream in an unpublished treatise entitled "Cargo Theology" as a collective daydream composed of conscious and unconscious materials — stories, images, clichés, group reactions, stereotypes, prejudices—all of which gave a community a consciousness of its identity. The modern city had such a mythdream, one that was mercantile and sterile. On the other hand the Latin American peoples and the peoples of the third world had a mythdream that was "hieratic, intuitive and affective": "The deepest springs of vitality in these races have been sealed up by the Conqueror and Colonizer, where they have not actually been poisoned by him. But if the stone is removed from the spring perhaps its waters will purify themselves by new life and regain their creative, fructifying power."[54]

Openness to nature was invariably a part of such successful communities. It was this element that gave man a view of the idyllic world that had always existed beneath the taut surface of civilized life. He was struck by the outlook of the Father Zosima in *The Brothers Karamazov* who was able to see the world as a paradise in spite of its treachery.[55] In *Mystics and Zen Masters* (1967) he contended that if approached with the right sort of vision the earth would yield "meaning, order, truth, and salvation."[56] "You start where you are," he observed, "you deepen what you already have, and you realize that you are already there . . . All we need is to experience what we already possess."[57] Given this alteration in vision, the world would awaken for man as it had for those primitive peoples whose heightened perceptions allowed them to see even the animals as living words in a cosmic vocabulary.[58] It is the paradisal motif in Merton's writing that balances the negative, ascetic elements in his vision.

The influence of Zen on Merton's paradisal outlook was decisive. He used Zen as a way of both transcending the world and valuing it in its limited state. With Zen there was no need to exclude from vision the riches of the physical world in order to focus the interior eye. It made no difference whatever, he wrote, if external objects were present in the mirror of consciousness. There was no need to exclude or suppress external objects because enlightenment "did not consist in being without them."[59] These external objects were absorbed in a vision of being, a void, which to Merton, with his characteristic enthusiasm, was not only not a mere negation, but was a *"pure affirmation* of the fullness of positive being."[60] This sense of fullness was what he meant by the ground of being — his *experiencing* of a unifying presence in nature. It involved allowing being in its full concreteness to fill the consciousness of the observer, permitting him to look out through being and through the creatures of the world as though fulfilling the role of consciousness not only for himself but for them also.

Merton felt some chagrin at the fact that such a vision had already been introduced to America in the nineteenth century by Emerson and Thoreau, but that it had not survived. Instead of the unsystematic, transcultural perception of Zen, American thought and behavior continued to be dominated by the heritage of Cartesian self-awareness, which assumed that the empirical ego was the starting point of an "infallible intellectual progress to truth and spirit, more and more refined, abstract, and immaterial."[61] Zen, on the other hand, freed one from "verbal formulas and linguistic preconceptions" and frustrated the mind that tried to wring a set of clear meaning from every creature and object.[62] The Zen "fact," he observed, "always lands across our road like a fallen tree beyond which we cannot pass."[63] He illustrated this insight vividly in terms of the Zen *koans* or stories:

> Many of the Zen stories, which are almost always incomprehensible in rational terms, are simply the ringing of an alarm clock, and the reaction of the sleeper. Usually the misguided sleeper makes a response which in effect turns off the alarm so that he can go back to sleep. Sometimes he jumps out of bed with a shout of astonishment that it is late. Sometimes he just sleeps and does not hear the alarm at all.[64]

Zen focused all of Merton's latent resistance to abstractionism by making it clear that the classifications and judgments that were the foundation of Western thought simply obscured the light. He symbolized this futile cerebration through the image of the "birds of appetite"—the predatory abstractionism that paralleled technology by exploiting and altering being instead of becoming attentive to it and resting against it.

The style of Merton's essays ranges from the lushness of "Hagia Sophia" (1962), which was included in *Emblems of a Season of Fury*, to the reportage technique which he used in *The Original Child Bomb* (1962). "Hagia Sophia" shows Merton in a moment of unrestrained lyricism. The piece is loosely structured around the cycle of the sun and of the monk's office — prayers, usually the Psalms, which were sung at various times during the day. The title "Hagia Sophia" (Holy Wisdom) was explained by Merton in a letter he wrote to the artist Victor Hammer in 1959. Hagia Sophia was the conception of God as Mother, the feminine principle in creation, the "dark, yielding, tender counterpart of the power, justice, creative dynamism of the Father."[65]

The piece is structured in such a way that the atmosphere of the liturgy and of the narrator's progress through the day are in the softest harmony. The frailty of man's condition is sounded at the outset in "Lauds." Merton imagines himself asleep in a hospital, awakened from his dream by the soft voice of a nurse, the feminine principle that he wanted to depict. He feels like "all mankind awakening," an emergence from "primordial nothingness" in which his sense of identity is dimly felt and precarious and in which the comforting touch of the nurse is therefore crucial. He senses "a hidden wholeness" as well as an "invisible fecundity" in the world.[66] The next section, "Prime," is set just after sunrise. It is the time of first consciousness, and the narrator makes some effort toward self-expression. "Lauds," which follows, is a time of feeling and absorbing. "Tierce" is sung during the fullness of morning and is almost ebulliently expressive, representing a time of exertion and maximum consciousness:

> The Sun burns in the sky like the Face of God, but we do not know his countenance as terrible. His light is diffused in the air and the light of God is diffused by Hagia Sophia. We do not see the Blinding One in black emptiness. He speaks to us gently in ten thousand things, in which His light is one fulness and one Wisdom. Thus He shines not on them but from within them.[67]

The liturgical cycle is completed with the saying of "Compline," in which night "embraces" the silent half of the earth and in which a "homeless" God, immanent in his cosmos but unrecognized in it, is an exile who "lies down in desolation under the sweet stars of the world and entrusts Himself to sleep,"[68] returning like other men to the formless, nameless world of night. The essay is marked by a fine delicacy and warmth.

Contrasted with the full lyricism of "Hagia Sophia," *The Original Child Bomb* is in low key. The book concerns the making and dropping of the first atomic bomb, a bomb whose newness caused the Japanese to name it, not without bitterness, the "original child" bomb. The book possesses an understated, ironic tone and macabre intensity. The language is simple, almost childlike, and factual:

> There was discussion about which city should ·be selected as the first target. Some wanted it to be Kyoto,

an ancient capital of Japan and a center of the Buddhist religion. Others said no, this would cause bitterness. As a result of a chance conversation, Mr. Stinson, the Secretary of War, had recently read up on the history and beauties of Kyoto. He insisted that this city should be left untouched.[69]

Merton was struck by the unconscious travesty of religion underlying the official scenario for the first bombrun. He describes this scenario with judicial equilibrium. The bomb, the "original child," is a burlesque of the Christ child. It is "tucked away" in the "womb" of the plane by airmen who were as "excited as little boys on Christmas Eve."[70] The original detonation of the bomb in New Mexico had the code name "Trinity." "Papacy" was the name given to the island from which the bomber took off. The account of the bombing is complemented by the black mat finish of the cover which gives the book a sarcophagus-like appearance. The incongruity between the horror of the bombing and the pious code chosen for it, whose ironies are so skillfully drawn out, makes *The Original Child Bomb* a devastating portrait of the hypocrisy and bankruptcy of Western policy and one of Merton's most powerful books.

One of Merton's most common techniques is to use themes from Greek mythology in order to provide a framework for a comment about contemporary culture. Heracleitos is used as a symbol of fiery dynamism and mutability. Prometheus is used as a symbol of man's desire to manage the universe, especially through technology. Juxtaposing the stories of Prometheus in Hesiod and Aeschylus, Merton wrote in *The Behaviour of Titans* (1961) that there were two faces of Prometheus representing two attitudes toward life. One of these expressed rebelliousness against an unpredictable cosmos and involved the remaking of it through technology; another expressed a Job-like forbearance followed by a final reconciliation with the world.[71]

He portrayed contemporary man as the rebellious, vindictive Prometheus. In thus seizing his freedom from the uncertainties of his environment, contemporary man paradoxically seized something that Merton felt had already been given to him but that he could not acknowledge, because he believed pessimistically that no god "would be willing to give it to him for nothing" (p. 19).

The most striking of those of Merton's essays framed by the Greek myths is "Atlas and the Fat Man," which was included in *The Behaviour of Titans*. In Hesiod Atlas stood at the western end of the known world holding up heaven and earth. In their mythology the Greeks eventually established his abode as a high North African mountain that was visible from the Mediterranean. Atlas is depicted as a "sentient mountain," a "high silent man of lava, with feet in the green surf, watching the stream of days and years" (p. 24). He holds the world together in "massive silence" except for the occasional utterance in the form of the "short bass clangor of a bell" (p. 25). Nature and time move in concert with the breathing of Atlas:

> When it is evening, when night begins to darken, when rain is warm in the summer darkness and rumors come up from the woods and from the banks of rivers, then shores and forests sound around you with a wordless solicitude of mothers. It is then that flowering palms enchant the night with their sweet smell. . . . In the sacred moment between sleeping and staying awake, Atlas speaks to the night as to a woman . . . He speaks of fires that night, and woman, do not understand. Green fires that are extinguished by intelligence, that night and woman possess. Golden fires of spirit that are in the damp warm rocky roots of the earth. White fires that are clear outside of earth and sky which night and woman cannot reach. (pp. 26-27)

The effect is exotically sensuous. Even the fat man, representing the bloated technocracy of the West, is submerged in the prevailing lyricism and dissolves into the misty dreams of Atlas, who stands patiently staring "with a cloud on his shoulder, watching the rising sun" (p. 48).

Circulating through Merton's essays are a number of dominant symbols, the most formidable of these being those of light and darkness. His use of the motifs of light and darkness is richly complex. If he depicts contemplation as a journey from darkness to light, he also depicts it — with conscious ambiguity — as a journey from light to darkness, a beckoning through an awesome darkness in which the naked soul comes into touch with God, who is experienced as a darkness more illuminating than light.

There are two kinds of darkness, the darkness of asceticism which blocks out the glare of the world and the darkness in which the interior man awakens to the fullness of reality. In this latter darkness the natural light of ordinary perception is of no more use, Merton wrote, than a flashlight to an owl when it is "dazzled by the light of high noon. The light of the sun blinds not only the owl but the flashlight."[72] The extinguishing of a lesser light in order that a purer light might shine in its place is a frequent theme in Merton. It is necessary to turn away from the "candlelight of our own desires and judgments," he wrote, in order to experience the "spiritual daylight" of God's presence.[73] Paradoxically, this greater light is often portrayed as a darkness. The reason is that it is a brilliant light that blinds the gazer. Moreover, having been brought into contact with infinity, the gazer feels in his solitude both afraid and doubtful when confronted with a new consciousness of the "black mirror" of his own soul.[74]

The eventual effect is to turn the contemplative's interior landscape into a "wasteland without special features of any kind," a darkness in which he lacks even the consolation of beholding a personal disaster.[75] "A cataclysm of the spirit," Merton added wryly, "if terrible, is also interesting."[76] It was this ebb in the contemplative's experience that gave rise to feelings of helplessness and inadequacy in which, wrote Merton, "we have nothing of our own to rely on, and nothing in our nature to support us, and nothing in the world to guide us or give us light."[77] Nevertheless, in this no man's land, the abject soul could suddenly be visited by flashes of "dark lightning" that lifted it into ecstasy—an image that reinforces Merton's paradoxical equation of light and darkness.[78] The final transmutation of the aspiring soul plunges it into an abyss of blazing light that is "pure darkness" to the mind and in which consciousness is transformed like a "bar of iron in the white heat of a furnace."[79]

Another symbolic motif is the emptying of life by itself. The filling of the soul by God empties it of its impurities and gives the contemplative an unexpected "thirst for emptiness, for selflessness," as Merton put it in *The Waters of Siloe* (1949).[80] It is a desert emptiness, involving a neutrality of spirit that leaves the soul "detached from earthly things and not yet in possession of those in heaven."[81] Riding the crest of such experience, the contemplative is moved in turn to empty himself, not only of his weaknesses, but of the riches of his vision, so that others might be filled.

Merton frequently used symbolism to unify his essays, which characteristically involved a series of loosely related observations. The symbolic motif is not necessarily visual. An example is his elaboration of the idea of *dread* in *The Climate of Monastic Prayer* (1969). The theme of dread is woven into the book so as to produce an underlying mood of uncertainty, humility, and challenge in the aspiring contemplative. Usually the unifying motifs are visual and arresting. An example occurs in the essay "Events and Pseudo-Events" in *Faith and Violence* (1968) in which he uses snake handling as practised by the mountain people of Tennessee and North Carolina as a visual focus for his discussion of the hypnotic handling of news events by the media.

Elaborate symbolic structuring can be seen in *The New Man* (1962). Although loosely associated, the essays in *The New Man* are fused through the use of the imagery of light, darkness, mirror, and fire. The book opens in darkness and closes in light. The initial somberness is caused by a "dark terror" that arises as the speaker considers the "foundering" life of modern man, who seems "ready with each breath to plunge into nothingness" and yet inexplicably remains "afloat on the void."[82] The stillness is broken only by the splash of those who, though bursting with life, plunge into the abyss dragging others after them. The mood holds until there is an awakening to a consciousness of the divine image within, which Merton saw as the key to man's identity.

The divine image is present in an "uncreated" state, "buried and concealed" in the darkness of the self (p. 167). It is uncreated in the sense that it has not yet become a conscious part of man's experience. If it fails to become integrated into experience, it is like a broken mirror, and the "torn and divided" self has somehow to overcome the "disintegrating force" of the illusions that blur its consciousness of its identity (p. 190). In this way the inner image can be made whole again, and the divine presence can fill the soul with its "light and its lineaments as though He were reflected in a mirror" (p. 206). Gradually, the divine image becomes a true likeness. The metaphor is extended through an analogy with photography: "A blurred photograph of a person is a picture or an image of the person, but it is overexposed or double-exposed or otherwise defective. A clear photograph is not only a picture of the person but is a 'likeness' of the person, giving an exact idea of him" (p. 61).

The discovery of one's true identity through the sharpened image of the self is accompanied by an infusion of inspirational zeal, which Merton conveys through the image of fire. *The New Man* ends in a celebration of the new light and the new fire, a light that "leaps" out of the darkness and a fire that mysteriously "comes from stone": "In the old days, on Easter night, the Russian peasants used to carry the blest fire home from Church. The light would scatter and travel in all directions through the darkness, and the desolation of the night would be pierced and dispelled as lamps came on in the windows of the farmhouses one by one. Even so the glory of God sleeps everywhere, ready to blaze out unexpectedly in created things" (pp. 242-243). The patterns of imagery are typical of Merton's approach to symbolism in that they are carefully interwoven and yet appear natural and incidental because of the way in which they are scattered informally throughout the writing.

Merton's gifts as an essayist are manifest: lucidity, fluidity, and an engaging conversational style. His essays on society continue to raise the question of whether or not he had overreached himself in moving to the public platform in the 1960s. It is in the moral and political analyses of particular social situations that he is most vulnerable, where the reader sometimes has a sense of his straying out of his depth. Nevertheless, his strength as a social commentator is undeniable. It lies in his ability to perceive the symbolic import of some important but overlooked events. In so doing he was often able to trace the outline of society's psyche with originality and with compelling persuasiveness and art.

In the late 1960s Merton decided to give up the kind of essay writing he had been doing, partly because of a growing disaffection with some of the social protest groups he had become identified with, but chiefly because he felt that it was time to stop trying to be an "authority on everything," as he confided to a friend in 1965.[83] He declared in the same year that he was moving toward semiretirement into a more "complete solitude." Any future writing would be on a much smaller scale, and it would be, he hoped, more personal and more creative than much of the work he had been doing.[84] There were books of essays already in the works, but increasingly after 1965 he turned his attention to journal writing and to poetry. As an essayist he had said what he had wanted to say—more, perhaps, than he had wanted to say. It was time to draw inward again.

Notes

[1]*Gestapo*, p.53.

[2]"First and Last Thoughts," in *A Thomas Merton Reader*, ed. Thomas P. McDonnell (New York, 1962), p.x.

[3]"Introduction" to *To Live is to Love* by Ernesto Cardenal (New York, 1972), p. 12.

[4]Letter to James Laughlin, Sept. 27, 1966.

[5]Letter to W. H. Ferry, Sept. 18, 1961.

[6]Letter to W. H. Ferry, April 30, 1965.

[7]Letter to Barbara Hubbard, Feb. 16, 1968.

[8]Letter to Margaret Randall de Mondragon, Jan. 27, 1963.

[9]"Events and Pseudo-Events," in *Faith and Violence* (Notre Dame, Indiana, 1968), p. 151.

[10]"Preface," Disputed Questions (New York, 1960), p. vii.

[11]*Faith and Violence*, p. 213.

[12]Letter to Edward Keating, April 7, 1964.

[13]*Faith and Violence*, p. 153.

[14]Notebook #55. The entry was dated Nov. 28, 1967.

[15]"The Time of the End is the Time of No Room," in *Raids on the Unspeakable* (New York, 1966), p. 70.

[16]David Steindal-Rast, "Recollections of Thomas Merton's Last Days in the West," *Monastic Studies*, VII (1969), p. 8.

[17]"A Tribute to Gandhi," in *Seeds of Destruction* (New York, 1964), p. 221.

[18]*Seeds of Destruction,* p. 12.

[19]"Preface" to the Japanese edition of *Seeds of Contemplation* (Tokyo, 1966), pp. 3-4. Manuscript.

[20]"Mount Athos," in *Disputed Questions,* p. 82.

[21]"The Ladder of Divine Ascent," *Jubilee,* VII (Feb., 1960), p. 37.

[22]"Love and Tao," in *Mystics and Zen Masters* (New York, 1967), p. 78.

[23]*The New Man* (New York, 1961), p. 104.

[24]Steindal-Rast, "Recollections of Thomas Merton's Last Days in the West," p. 7.

[25]*Faith and Violence,* p. 118.

[26]Letter to Mrs. A. K. Coomaraswamy, Jan. 13, 1961.

[27]Letter to Thomas Congdon, Sept. 25, 1966.

[28]"A Letter to Pablo Antonio Cuadra Concerning Giants," in *Emblems of a Season of Fury* (New York, 1963), p. 80.

[29]"Final Integration: Toward a 'Monastic Therapy,'" in *Contemplation in a World of Action* (New York, 1971), p. 211.

[30]Letter to Miguel Grinberg, Aug. 16, 1964.

[31]Thomas P. McDonnell, "An Interview with Thomas Merton," *Motive,* XXVII (Oct., 1967), p. 36.

[32]*Contemplation in a World of Action,* p. 222.

[33]*Thoughts in Solitude* (New York, 1958), pp. 19-20.

[34]*The Wisdom of the Desert: Sayings from the Desert Fathers of the Fourth Century* (New York, 1960), p. 7.

[35]*Thoughts in Solitude,* p. 26.

[36]Frederick Joseph Kelly, *Man before God: Thomas Merton on Social Responsibility* (New York, 1974), p. 262.

[37]"Answers on Art," in *Raids on the Unspeakable,* p. 172.

[38]*The Ascent to Truth* (New York, 1951), p. 21.

[39]*Seeds of Contemplation* (Norfolk, Conn., 1949), p. 91. Subsequent references will be incorporated in the text.

[40]"First and Last Thoughts," p. viii.

[41]Y. H. Krikorian, "The Fruits of Mysticism," *New Republic,* CXXI (Sept. 12, 1949), p. 17.

[42]*New Seeds of Contemplation* (New York, 1961), p. 87. Subsequent references will be incorporated in the text.

[43]"Letter to an Innocent Bystander," in *The Behaviour of Titans* (New York, 1961), p. 64.

[44]*Disputed Questions,* p. x.

[45]*Seasons of Celebration* (New York, 1965), p. 20.

[46]*Conjectures of a Guilty Bystander* (New York, 1966), p. 16.

[47]Michele Murray, "Thomas Merton, The Public Monk," *National Catholic Reporter,* XXX (Dec. 21, 1966), p. 9.

[48]*Raids on the Unspeakable*, p. 46.
[49]Letter to W. H. Ferry, April 11, 1967.
[50]"Preface" to the Vietnamese edition of *No Man is an Island* (Saigon, 1967). Manuscript.
[51]"The Sacred Ciy." *The Center Magazine*, I (1968), p. 77.
[52]*Raids on the Unspeakable*, p. 10.
[53]"The Street is for Celebration," *The Mediator*, XX (Summer, 1969), p. 3.
[54]"A Letter to Pablo Antonio Cuadra concerning Giants," in *Emblems of a Season of Fury* (New York, 1963), p. 78.
[55]"Wisdom in Emptiness," in *New Directions in Prose and Poetry*, ed. James Laughlin, XVII (1961), p. 81.
[56]*Mystics and Zen Masters*, p. 111.
[57]Steindal-Rast, "Recollections of Thomas Merton's Last Days in the West," pp. 2-3.
[58]Notebook #86. The entry is dated Sept. 17, 1967.
[59]*Mystics and Zen Masters*, p. 27.
[60]Ibid., p. 27.
[61]Ibid., p. 26.
[62]*Zen and the Birds of Appetite* (New York, 1968), p. 44.
[63]Ibid., p. 51.
[64]Ibid., p. 50.
[65]Letter to Victor Hammer, May 14, 1959.
[66]"Hagia Sophia," in *Emblems of a Season of Fury*, pp. 61-63.
[67]Ibid., pp. 64-65.
[68]Ibid., p. 69.
[69]*The Original Child Bomb: Points for Meditation to be Scratched on the Walls of a Cave* (New York, 1962). Entry No. 7. The book is unpaginated.
[70]Ibid., No. 26.
[71]*The Behaviour of Titans*, pp. 13-14. Subsequent references will be incorporated in the text.
[72]*Ascent to Truth*, p. 263.
[73]"Light in Darkness," in *Disputed Questions*, p. 213.
[74]*Bread in the Wilderness* (New York, 1953), p. 122.
[75]"St. John of the Cross," in *Saints for Now*, ed. Clare Boothe Luce (New York, 1952), pp. 256-257.
[76]Ibid., pp. 256-257.
[77]*Seeds of Contemplation*, p. 172.
[78]*Bread in the Wilderness*, p. 119.
[79]*Ascent to Truth*, p. 261.
[80]*The Waters of Siloe* (New York, 1949), p. 3.
[81]"St. John of the Cross," p. 257.

[82]*The New Man* (New York, 1961), pp. 3-4. Subsequent references will be incorporated in the text.
[83]Letter to Claire Livingston, Dec. 12, 1965.
[84]Letter to Frank Dell'Isola, June 9, 1965.

Poet

WHEN MERTON ENTERED THE contemplative life, he burned most of the novels he had written, but, significantly, he kept the poems. Considering the brush-off he was to receive from literary critics (with the notable exception of some early praise from Robert Lowell), he must have wondered at times about his faith in his poetic powers. Some of the reviews he received were mercilessly perfunctory. In a succinct review of *The Strange Islands* (1957), for example, W. S. Merwin confessed that "what poetry there may be in the book" was beyond his appreciation.[1] It was the late 1960s and early 1970s before Merton's poetry received any sort of adulation from the establishment press, principally because of the impact of his final poems. Some of the earlier poems appeared in a respectable anthology in 1965, and there he found himself for the first time in the company of his peers.[2]

If American literati were slow to recognize Merton, that delay did not seem to affect the volume of his publication. New Directions printed his work loyally from his first book of poems until his death, and his publisher James Laughlin was helpful in putting him in touch with important poets in the New Directions lineup. In this way he began to correspond with people like Lawrence Ferlinghetti, Kenneth Patchen, and William Everson (Brother Antoninus) and from there was led to an acquaintance with other poets. He wrote to and met with Denise Levertov and Wendell Berry, and he came into contact with some young Louisville poets in the 1960s.

In one of his taped lectures Merton said that he believed he lived in an age of good poetry, and he did his best, finally, to catch up with what was going on.[3] He became attracted to the "beat" poets — Ginsberg, Kerouac, Ferlinghetti, and Corso. He liked both the egalitarian spirit of the beats and their style, a spontaneous outpouring from the unconscious. He found the beats a relief from what seemed to him to be the stifling academic style that had overtaken recent American verse. He referred to these poets as the "esoteric American pontiffs of the day"[4] and noted regretfully that they seemed to spend much of their time "cutting each other up," an observation that was reinforced by painful experience.[5] He believed that the academic poets were caught in a sterile impasse in which they were reduced to experimenting with language instead of writing a poetry that was meaningful. He abhorred didacticism, and yet he also disliked an arid emphasis on technique. He described the sort of balance he wanted in a rather cryptic letter to his poet friend Robert Lax: "never try to say nothing in a poem (i say): only see it doesn't say nothing wrong. There ought to be a lot more poems (i say) only they shouldn't say so many wrong things, this must all be stopped. more poems, but not so many words and things like that."[6] He wanted a poetry that was spiritually meaningful and he found himself turning to the poets of other cultures, especially those in Latin America.

It is difficult to know what special role Merton assigned to poetic art. In one of his notebooks he wrote that the essential quality of poetry was that it was "useless," thereby distinguishing it from his essay writing.[7] In one of the taped lectures he differentiated poetry from prose principally on the basis of rhythm, feeling that it was chiefly rhythm that reached beneath the cerebral life of the reader to the depths of his affective life.[8]

Some of Merton's earliest poems were published by Victor Hammer in 1971.[9] Of interest perhaps to the hardy literary historian, the poems are rather undistinguished, uneven, and derivative, reflecting his reading of Wordsworth, Blake, Hopkins, Eliot, Joyce, and Lorca. In a rather tangled way they point to some of the themes that were to preoccupy him later on. The *Thirty Poems* (1944), which came out as part of New Directions' "Poets of the Year" series, marks a real beginning in Merton's career as a poet. There are derivative lines, as in "The Flight into Egypt" with its echoes of Blake's "London," but the poems are fresh and distinctive for the most part. The thirty poems were part of a group of poems that had been entrusted to Mark Van Doren when Merton entered the monastery. Van Doren thus made the selection. The poems had been composed in Greenwich Village, at St. Bonaventure University in Olean, N.Y., and at the Abbey of Gethsemani. Merton recalled vividly the circum-

stances surrounding the composition of some of the Greenwich
Village poems:

> I would get an idea, and walk around the streets, among
> the warehouses, towards the poultry market at the foot of
> Twelfth Street, and I would go out on the chicken dock
> trying to work out four lines of verse in my head, and sit
> in the sun. And after I had looked at the fireboats and the
> old empty barges and the other loafers and the Stevens
> Institute on its bluff across the river in Hoboken, I would
> write the poem down on a piece of scrap paper and go
> home and type it out.[10]

Merton's memory of his time at St. Bonaventure's is equally
evocative. Out of his window he would look beyond the chapel
to the garden, the fields, and the woods. "My eyes often wandered out there," he recalled, "and rested in that peaceful
scene," and as the months went on "I began to drink poems out
of those hills."[11] Poems from this period include "The Flight into
Egypt," "Song for Our Lady of Cobre," "An Argument: Of the
Passion of Christ," which appeared in *Thirty Poems,* and "Ariadne at the Labyrinth" and "The Man in the Wind," which along
with some others from 1940 to 1941 came out later in *A Man in the
Divided Sea.* A hitherto unnoticed letter, which was sent to a
graduate student in 1951 by a monk who was acting as Merton's
secretary, dates the early poems, revealing that most of them
were composed in 1941.[12] Merton's poetic fertility at this time
coincided with the excitement that preceded his decision about
the shape that his life would take; he entered Gethsemani toward
the end of 1941. He would not be such a prolific writer of poetry
again until the later 1960s, when he decided to wind down his
involvement in other kinds of writing and duties.

   Although a modest press run, all copies of the *Thirty Poems*
were sold. In spite of this apparent success, Robert Lowell noted
that Merton's poetry had "attracted almost no attentive criticism" and concluded that the "poet would appear to be more
phenomenal than the poetry."[13] Merton liked many of these
early poems, and he included a number of them in the *Selected*

Poems, which came out in 1959. The thirty poems divide readily into secular and religious subjects. Their range is limited; there is little sign of the presence of the larger society, except perhaps for faint echoes of the war in "Lent in a Time of War" and in "The Dark Morning." It was an enclosed world on the whole. As far as the religious verse was concerned, he appears to have had hopes for himself as a renovator of this sort of poetry, writing to a journal in 1941 that he was tired of "well-intentioned, fairly commonplace, half-sentimental" religious poetry and calling for an authentic poetry that was "profoundly mystical."[14]

The poems are formally structured for the most part, the best ones, like "Lent in a Time of War," being compact and tense. The formality came from Merton's interest in the metaphysical poetry of the seventeenth century. Of the metaphysical poems, "An Argument: Of the Passion of Christ" and "The Blessed Virgin Mary Compared to a Window," which was indebted to Donne's "Of My Name in the Window," are conspicuous examples.

"An Argument: Of the Passion of Christ" was written in tight quatrains set in rhyming tetrameter. Most of the poem is a euphemistic, rather abstract account of the wages of sin. There are some striking moments, though, as in the lines that project the stigma of sin into the world of the fetus:

> The furious prisoner of the womb,
> Rebellious, in the jaws of life,
> Learns, from the mother's conscious flesh,
> The secret laws of blood and strife.[15]

In "The Blessed Virgin Mary Compared to a Window" the central conceit, which is contained in the title, is handled with deftness. Like the window, the Virgin is a medium through which the divine light passes into the world. When the sun (God) shines through her, her own character, like the glass in the window, disappears, and one sees only the light: "I vanish into day, and leave no shadow" (*CP*, p. 47). Even the grille of the window is used to elaborate the conceit, as the Virgin is said to leave no shadow but "the geometry of my cross/ Whose frame and structure are the strength/ By which I die." The punning on light, sun, and Son are typical of Merton's early poems.

The poetry is heightened by the pyrotechnics of surrealism, inspired by the Spanish poet Lorca, who is the subject of one of the thirty poems. Merton was fond of interchanging the senses in a synesthetic manner in order to "pair them off unnaturally" so that the "eye hears, the ear feels, the lip sees."[16] The effect is observable in "The Sponge Full of Vinegar," in which the Roman soldiers beneath the cross are pictured as gambling in the "clash of lancelight" (CP, p. 57). The infiltration of sound into the image is both original and convincing and was an early sign of Merton's power.

Merton's taped lectures reveal a strong interest in the use of sound. In discussing Rilke's poem "The Panther," for example, he read the poem in German so that his students might get the sound before translating it into English in order to get the meaning. The army major in "Lent in a Time of War" is largely a creation of sound, a man composed of "cord and catskin" who never "dreams his eyes may come to life and thread/ The needle-light of famine in a waterglass" (CP, p. 27). The high-pitched "i" and "e" sounds intensify the feeling of acuteness appropriate to the crises of war and famine, while the image of the "needle-light" works at the same effect visually.

Merton cultivated unexpected combinations of words — as in the "singing desert" in "The Flight into Egypt" (CP, p. 28). In pursuit of an effect of controlled anarchy, he used the imagery of disorder to generate a sense of the primal, inchoate world of the subconscious. An example is his poem "Saint Jason," whose density is further enhanced by its welding of Greek mythology and Christian eschatology:

> This is the night the false Saint Jason
> Wakes in fear from his cannibal sleep,
> And drenches the edges of his eyes
> With his tears' iron overflow;
>
> For the flying scream of his dead woman
> Opened the stitches of his skin,
> And Jason bounced in the burly wind
> Like a man of sack and string. (CP, p. 31)

The early poems are most effective when Merton concentrates on the richness of his own experience, as is seen in the tender lines he composed on hearing that his brother had been reported missing in action:

Sweet brother, if I do not sleep
My eyes are flowers for your tomb;
And if I cannot eat my bread,

My fasts shall live like willows where you died.
If in the heat I find no water for my thirst,
My thirst shall turn to springs for you, poor traveller.
(CP, pp. 35-36)

The poems are most successful when they are set in an exact and familiar locale. Some of the poems emerge vividly from their backgrounds, like "The Trappist Abbey: Matins" with its mournful Kentucky train whistle. Similarly, "Aubade: Lake Erie" is set firmly in the vicinity of Olean, New York, where Merton taught in 1941. The aubade is a lyric sung at dawn, a favorite time for Merton, a time of change and potential renewal. In spite of the strained comparison of the vine-covered fields of New York with the "sweet leafage of an artificial France," the poem submits to its locale on the whole, especially in the images of the "Indian water," the "hay-colored sun," the "western freight," and the "gap-toothed grin of factories" in the distance (CP, p. 35). The juxtaposition of the children, whose "shining voices" play like "churchbells over the field," and the dusky vagabonds who rouse themselves reluctantly and head for the industrial wasteland over the horizon is typical of Merton's early poetry. These were his songs of innocence and experience.

"Song for Our Lady of Cobre" delicately reflects the colors of its Cuban setting with its flood of sunlight and large water birds. The poem is about the mixing of the white and black races in Cuba, but withholds a direct social, moral, or political statement of its subject. Instead, the prevailing viewpoint is aesthetic:

The white girls lift their heads like trees,
The black girls go
Reflected like flamingoes in the street.

The white girls sing as shrill as water,
The black girls talk as quiet as clay.

The white girls open their arms like clouds,
The black girls close their eyes like wings. (*CP*, pp. 29-30)

The effect of the graceful sensuality of the scene is to bring out equally the beauty of both white and black girls, an impression that is so strong that it makes any other sort of view that one might take of them seem petty. The splendour of the poem lies in its affirmation of the beauty of each race, separately as well as in unison, without suppressing the characteristics that are proper to each, the colors of the flamingo and clay uniting harmoniously with the white of the clouds. The poem is further enhanced by the simplicity and dignity of its language and rhythm.

A *Man in the Divided Sea* came out in 1946. The title was drawn from the Israelites' miraculous crossing of the Red Sea, an acknowledgement of Merton's gratitude at having escaped the grasp of a meretricious culture. It also expressed the dualism underlying the book's themes, which are both secular and religious. The secular poems cover a small number of themes, though these are conveyed through a myriad of images. Merton's extravagant use of similes derives in part from the incongruous conditions under which he composed some of these early poems. The poem "April," for example, which ostensibly dealt with nature, was written under the stimulus of the rush and congestion of New York City. "I thought it up," he recalled, "weaving in and out of the crowds . . . in and out of the light and the shade of the Forties, between Fifth and Sixth avenues."[17]

The collection reveals Merton as more of an innovator than did the *Thirty Poems*. In the "Song" from "Crossportion's Pastoral," for example, he experiments freely with language. In a letter he wrote in 1966, he explained that he coined the word *crossportion*, meaning by it "one who has taken the cross for his portion," adding that the poem was part of a larger lost sequence that he had written in the 1930s.[18] The poem's surrealistic landscape —

"The bottom of the sea has come/ And builded in my noiseless room" — gave him the opportunity to experiment not only with picture, sound, and diction, but also with syntax.[19] A bedroom is described as "unroom sleep some other where," a syntactical dislocation that conveys a sense of suspension that is an important part of the poem's atmosphere.

He used this sort of syntactical experimentation sparingly, though tellingly, setting it off by surrounding it with more conventional language. In "The Bombarded City" there is a dream-like feeling of redolence and decay. The image of the foreground is sharp and yet inexplicable — a mysterious "lunar wood" that merges with the picture of a ghostly cenotaph with its "white geometry of peace" (CP, pp. 75-76). The feeling of dislocation intensifies as Merton focuses on the harvest of the war dead and on the power brokers who had incited the wars:

For even when field flowers shall spring
Out of the Leader's lips, and open eyes,
And even while the quiet root
Shall ravel his murdering brain,
Let no one, even on that holiday,
Forget the never-sleeping curse.
And even when the grass grows in his groin,
And golden-rod works in his rib,
And in his teeth the ragweed grins,
As furious as ambition's diligence. (CP, p. 77)

The images in A Man in the Divided Sea, rather like apparitions, float on the surface of the poems rather than emerging from prepared settings. The effect is often dramatic and exciting, even if occasionally mannered. The image of the child is one of the most entrenched of these symbols. In poems like the "Dirge For a Town in France" in A Man in the Divided Sea and "Evening" in Thirty Poems Merton focused on the enchantment of the child's world. Although aware that the vision of children yielded quickly to the anxieties and compulsion to conform that impinged on them from every side, he used the state of childhood to symbolize the free, responsive relationship with the world that he felt was available to everyone and that he believed he himself had attained. The fragrance of the child's vision is evocatively present in the poem "Evening," in which the children hear the moon speak to the hill and listen as the "wheatfields make their simple music,/ Praise the quiet sky" (CP, p. 41).

Many of the poems in *A Man in the Divided Sea* deal with Greek themes, some of these being among the most distinctive poems in the book. Ever since his father had read him stories from Greek mythology, Merton felt he had used these stories unconsciously as the basis of a "religion and of a philosophy" that he later recognized as underlying his intellectual formation.[20] The Greek poems balance the Christian poems as twin pillars in his thought and outlook. As opposed to the austerity of the Christian lyrics, the Greek poems are ripe and sensual, as in "Ariadne:"

> Behind the bamboo blinds,
> Behind the palms,
> In the green sundappled apartments of her palace
> Redslippered Ariadne, with a tiny yawn,
> Tosses a ball upon her roulette wheel. (CP, p. 63)

Merton's aestheticism fed on the luxuriance of the Greek myths. "The Greek Women" opens with this softened portrait:

> The ladies in red capes and golden bracelets
> Walk like reeds and talk like rivers,
> And sigh, like Vichy water, in the doorways.
>
> All spine and sandal stand the willow women;
> They shake their silver bangles
> In the olive-light of clouds and windows. (CP, p. 73)

The mood of reverie and indolence is broken as the women are suddenly called "widow women," whose men lie dead in the "alien earth" of Troy. The poem gathers in intensity, the images tightening as Merton focuses on one of the women, Clytemnestra, who had been unfaithful to Agamemnon, one of those who will be returning from Troy:

117

Beads and bracelets gently knifeclash all about her,
Because the conqueror, the homecome hero,
The soldier Agamemnon,
Bleeds in her conscience, twisting like a root. (*CP*, p. 74)

Merton skillfully used the bleeding in Clytemnestra's "conscience" as both a sign of guilt and an unsettling foreshadowing
of the impending murder of Agamemnon. He relied on the Greek
myths to provide him with elevated and coherent models of
experience with which to contrast the banality and fragmentation of contemporary life.

Merton's handling of the contemporary scene in *A Man in the
Divided Sea* is pointed and graphic, notably in "Aubade — The
City," "Aubade—Harlem," and "The Ohio River—Louisville."
The influence of Hart Crane is perceptible in "Aubade — The
City" in the description of Brooklyn Bridge with its "choiring
cables." For Merton, as for Crane, New York was *the* city, the
archetype of the modern city, for better or for worse. Both saw it
as a Dantean inferno inhabited by repressed inhabitants who
moved about like captive wolves. In "Aubade — The City" the
buildings have "faces" and the elevator doors "clash like
swords" (*CP*, pp. 86-87). Even the organic world, twisted out of
shape by urbanization, is intimidating. The sunlight, ordinarily
a ubiquitous symbol of hope in Merton, seeks out those who lurk
in their apartments, inducing paranoia.

In "Aubade — Harlem" Merton portrays the black tenements
— the "keyless aviaries" — with imagistic objectivity, balancing
the misery of Harlem against the affluent but equally desperate
situation of the whites who inhabit the "cells of whiter buildings," their psychiatric suffering played off against the physical
hardships endured by the blacks (*CP*, pp. 82-83).

"The Ohio River — Louisville," a later poem, shows a further
darkening of Merton's vision of the city. The river, used as a
sewage basin by the cities along it, is a symbol of the obliteration
of nature by urban life. The waterfront is dominated by the
"towering bridge, the crawling train," and the "sky-swung cables" of the derricks (*CP*, p. 79). Louisville is a tintype of the New
York skyline and thus a symbol of the endless duplication of such

scenes throughout America. The Ohio River was still clean enough for swimmers in the early 1940s, but the swimmers whom Merton overhears offer little relief from the industrialized gloom. These swimmers

> . . . float like alligators,
> And with their eyes as dark as creosote
> Scrutinize the murderous heat,
> Only there is anything heard:
> The thin, salt voice of violence,
> That whines, like a mosquito, in their simmering blood.
> (*CP*, p. 80)

One of Merton's most electrifying passages, the scene captures the latent racial violence of the border state, and regionalizes the mood through the word "creosote." The word refers to the coated pilings along the river front, but it is also the material with which Kentucky tobacco farmers paint their barns in order to promote drying and curing. The provocative sharpness of the imagery makes the poem a memorable example of Merton's early work.

The religious poems in *A Man in the Divided Sea* lack the daring of the city poems, but they do represent an advance over the *Thirty Poems*. The best are rooted in Merton's own experience, poems like "After the Night Office — Gethsemani Abbey" and, to a lesser extent, "The Trappist Cemetery — Gethsemani." The least effective are those that somewhat stalely reflect Merton's sifting of the vocabulary of his spiritual reading. In the most successful poems one encounters the figure of the new monk directly, the triumph of the man who had found his place in the scheme of things.

"After the Night Office — Gethsemani" is an example. Merton's finely tinted portrait of his fellow monks is enhanced by an astute structuring that brings out the heavenly paradox underlying their nocturnal lives. The scene is carefully laid. It is a "grey and frosty time," a time when the monastery barns "ride out of the night like ships" (*CP*, p. 108). He looks at the file of monks who, "bearing lanterns,/ Sink in the quiet mist," and reflects that these contemplatives who sank deeply into prayer during the night hours had their "noon" before dawn. The coming of dawn transfers the flood of light from within the monks outward to the "lances of the morning" that shower "all their gold against the steeple and the water-tower." At this point the monks are pictured as moving out of themselves in order to do their work. He concludes: "We find our souls all soaked in grace, like Gideon's fleece" (CP, p. 109). The poem's color, serenity, and tenderness make it one of the most appealing lyrics.

Figures for an Apocalypse (1947) does not measure up to A Man in the Divided Sea on the whole, but it does offer some interesting innovations in style. One of the book's principal problems is its declamatory style. Merton later traced the problem to his infatuation with the style of Leon Bloy, an influence that he felt made the indignation in the poems too "automatic."[21] The long title poem set the tone for the collection. Merton appears to have hoped that the power implicit in his apocalyptic vision would rub off on the poetry. What happens instead is that a shrill and loud tone drowns much of the book. His method in the title poem is that of a loose collage, a heady synthesis of biblical and secular images punctuated by a vision of the fall of New York — the modern Babylon. The versification is freer than in the earlier, formal poems, even if that freedom sometimes amounts to license.

The imagery in Figures for an Apocalypse is adventurously imaginative. The description of a row of theater marquees in "A Letter to America" — "the movies grit/ Their white electric teeth" — is typical.[22] With his bent toward surrealism, Merton was fascinated by the metamorphosis of imagery and seemed to enjoy the friction that resulted when one image changed into another with great speed. In "Theory of Prayer" we are told that the things that we say turn and betray us, writing the "names of our sins on flesh and bone/ In lights as hard as diamonds" (CP, p. 180). In "Evening: Zero Weather" the "lone" world is seen to be "streaky as a wall of marble/ With veins of clear and frozen snow" against a background in which the "bare fields" are as "silent as eternity" (CP, p. 174). The shuttling between matter and spirit was not only technically interesting to Merton, but a sign of his belief in the continuity underlying these ostensibly discrete worlds.

Some of the images appear contrived as in the lover in "Theory of Prayer" who, caught "in the loop of his own lie/ Strangles like a hare" (*CP*, p. 179). Other images are fresh and convincing, like the "ox-eyed land" in "Canticle for the Blessed Virgin" that mirrors the wintry configuration of Merton's Kentucky landscape with its patches of small lakes (*CP*, p. 161). Equally arresting is the image of the bulls in "Spring: Monastery Farm" roaming in their pens and singing "like trains" (*CP*, p. 169).

Some of the shorter poems show Merton's fondness for wit and paradox. In "Three Postcards from the Monastery," a title that he drew from Wallace Stevens, the world that he had left behind is portrayed as a huge blankness filled with "unidentified facades," much as one might expect a monastery to look. Paradoxically, it is the outside world that is marked by "penitential tunnels" and "non-entity," a world in which people veil their "elusive faces" in an ironic imitation of the monk's cowl (*CP*, pp. 153-155). Those in the monastery on the other hand are characterized as affluent recipients of a lavish nature that fills their "hands with gold," even though they had "fled to the penniless hills." Turning their backs on the "fatal fortunes" of the city, the contemplatives "inherit the world" and have enough left over to buy "Andromeda" (*CP*, p. 154.) In "The Sowing of Meanings" the energy of God is ingeniously portrayed as so vast and volatile that it has to be sown in "seed and root and blade and flower" in order to be contained and made manageable. The effect is a world surcharged with beauty and power too "terrible" to bear, so that the "wild countryside, unknown, unvisited of men" bears "sheaves of clean, transforming fire" that in turn surcharge the observer (*CP*, p. 188).

The Tears of the Blind Lions (1949) is a slimmer volume than its predecessors, containing only seventeen poems. This paucity was a reflection of Merton's increased workload and of his scruples about the usefulness of poetry to the life of contemplation. He rated the book highly in comparison with *Figures for an Apocalypse* and recognized its superior handling of tone as well as its greater conciseness, both of which he retained without having to give up his attachment to free verse. Two of the poems, "St. Malachy" and "From the Legend of St. Clement," received half of the Harriet Monroe Memorial Prize for 1949.

There are occasional lapses in taste, in the far-fetched prenatal description of John the Baptist, for example, but the general impression is of a more direct, more concise, and more vigorous poetry than in the previous volume. The mood of celibate joy is especially attractive: "When psalms surprise me with their music/ And antiphons turn to rum/ The Spirit sings."[23] There are few innovations in theme, but there is an increased attention to structuring. A good example is "Dry Places," in which Merton daringly paints a picture of an abandoned mining town overlaid on the biblical desert of austerity, madness, and demonic temptation. The isolation and menace are hauntingly emphasized:

> . . . the dusk
> Is full of lighted beasts
> And the mad stars preach wars without end:
> Whose bushes and grasses live without water,
> There the skinny father of hate rolls in his dust
> And if the wind should shift one leaf
> The dead jump up and bark for their ghosts. (*CP*, p. 216)

The imagery is original and coordinated, the image of the dead barking being especially effective in dramatizing the metaphysical evil and terror of the place. The atmosphere of delirium is richly ambiguous, since if the tendency to hallucinate evil is compelling, so is the underlying reality of evil in the town.

The Tears of the Blind Lions reflects an accomplished blending of Merton's religious sensibility and poetic craft. Poems like "The Reader" effectively convey both the hard surface and inner vitality of his experience:

> I sit hooded in this lectern
> Waiting for the monks to come,
> I see the red cheeses, and bowls
> All smile with milk in ranks upon their tables.
>
> Light fills my proper glove
> (I have won light to read by
> With a little, tinkling chain)

And the monks come down the cloister
With robes as voluble as water. (*CP*, p. 202)

He had simplified his poems and made them more direct, not
only by concentrating on the details of his own experience but
also by stripping from his writing the layers of similes which had
cluttered earlier volumes.

"St. Malachy" is another example of Merton's ability to inte-
grate his spirituality and religious observances with his poetic
perceptions. The poem dramatizes the seasonal impact of the
saint's feast day on the liturgical cycle:

In November, in the days to remember the dead
When air smells cold as earth,
St. Malachy, who is very old, gets up,
Parts the thin curtain of trees and dawns upon our land.
(*CP*, pp. 209-210)

The sharpness in focus brings out the power that had always
been latent in Merton's poetry but that had been diluted in some
of the earlier poems by excesses in diction and looseness in
structuring.

Eight years elapsed before the appearance of *The Strange Islands* (1957). The gap reflected Merton's increased workload and
his concentration on prose writing. Most of the poems in *The
Strange Islands* were written in 1955 and 1956. He wrote to Mark
Van Doren that something new was beginning to come out in his
work but that he was worried about glibness.[24] He was not the
only one. In reviewing *The Strange Islands* James Dickey com-
mented that Merton was "betrayed by his complacency."[25] There
were obviously poems that should have been omitted, especially
"Sports without Blood," an expressionistic, fragmentary poem
about the death of a Cambridge cricketer. Writing in the *Saturday
Review*, Donald Hall wondered in connection with some of the
weaker poems if Merton was capable of the sort of self-criticism
that would enable him to carry out adequate revisions of his
poetry.[26]

The question is an unavoidable one. The matter of revision can be illustrated in the case of "A Prelude: for the Feast of St. Agnes," which was a revision of a poem that had appeared in *The Sign of Jonas*.[27] Lines from this poem appear to have provided the title for *The Strange Islands* – "Come home, come home, old centuries/ Whose soundless islands ring me from within."[28] There are alterations in phrasing from the first to the second version, but these were minor. "O centuries" was replaced by "old centuries," and "this winter morning's iris" became "a winter morning's iris." Some of the changes are retrogressive. "The cities cry like peacocks in their sleep" gave way to the more blurred and indecisive line: "The cities cry, perhaps, like peacocks."

Merton's revisions were frequently nominal. He did not trust himself to revise well, feeling that he worked best under the initial heat of inspiration. In the 1960s, for example, he submitted a poem entitled "First Lesson about Man" to John Ciardi at the *Saturday Review*. Ciardi eventually printed the poem, but wanted the ending changed. Merton complied, though he refused to do so in the case of another poem — "With the World in My Bloodstream" — which Ciardi felt should have been more concise. The original ending of "First Lesson About Man" read:

> Man is the saddest animal
> He begins in zoology
> And that is where he generally
> Ends.

Merton changed this to read:

> Man is the saddest animal
> He begins in zoology
> And gets lost
> In his own bad news.[29]

His wariness about revision seems vindicated in this instance. In comparison with the cohesiveness of the original phrasing the revised ending intrudes somewhat roughly into the poem, the motif of "bad news" introducing a new and distracting element into it.

The Strange Islands shows Merton moving toward a freer colloquialism, bringing him more into line with contemporary verse. He also experimented with different line lengths in order to build into the poems the hollows of silence that he felt were essential to poetry, in which the reader was compelled to stop, be silent, and absorb the hidden meanings. "In Silence" manifests his experimentation with sound as well as structure. The poem centers on the speaker's perceptions of stones in a wall:

> Be still
> Listen to the stones of the wall.
> Be silent, they try
> To speak your
> Name. (*CP*, p. 280)

The lines were shortened and the progress of the poem made halting in order to trace the shape of individual stones as well as to create the pauses that would induce the sort of meditative reading that Merton wanted.

At one point the speaker's attempt to concentrate fails, and he finds himself questioning the "living" walls:

> Who are you?
> Who
> Are you? Whose
> Silence are you?
>
> Who (be quiet)
> Are you (as these stones
> Are quiet). (*CP*, pp. 280-281)

The speaker's failure, brought about by the inquisitive fluttering of his mind, disturbs the tranquil mood of the poem, but also creates dramatic interest. The speaker's perception of the stones has caught fire, a sign of that surcharging of the imagination that can be seen in Merton's poetry when the power and radiance of being are fully apprehended — even in blocks of stone:

> The stones
> Burn, even the stones
> They burn me. How can a man be still or
> Listen to all things burning? How can he dare
> To sit with them when
> All their silence
> Is on fire? (*CP*, p. 281)

The Strange Islands contains a number of poems about urban blight. The prophetic tone of these poems signals an increased aggressiveness in Merton's approach. "How to Enter a Big City" is an example:

> Lights tick in the middle.
> Blue and white steel
> Black and white
> People hurrying along the wall.
>
> The buildings, turning twice about the sun,
> Settle in their respective positions. (*CP*, pp. 225-226)

The tone of the poem becomes bitter as Merton considers the inhabitants of Louisville who come out into the light of the afternoon covered in "black powder,/ And begin to attack one another with statements." Marginally refreshed by a breeze off the river that "wipes the flies" from his "Kentucky collarbone," he reflects morosely on the betrayal of America's promise:

> The ghosts of historical men
> (Figures of sorrow and dust)
> Weep along the hills like turpentine.
> And seas of flowering tobacco
> Surround the drowning sons of Daniel Boone. (*CP*, p. 228)

The right arm of technocracy is war, represented in *The Strange Islands* by "The Guns of Fort Knox." The proximity of Merton's monastery to this large military base constituted an irony that persistently aroused him:

> Guns at the camp (I hear them suddenly)
> Guns make the little houses jump. I feel
> Explosions in my feet, through boards.
> Wars work under the floor. Wars
> Dance in the foundations. Trees
> Must also feel the guns they do not want
> Even in their core. (*CP*, p. 228)

Even the monastery hills reverberate, shifting their feet "in friable stone."

Impinged upon by the withering touch of technology, Merton turned as usual to nature, as in "Nocturne:"

> Night has a sea which quenches the machine
> Or part of it. Night has tides of rain
> And sources which go on
> Washing our houses when we turn to dream. (*CP*, p. 229)

In addition to the new subject matter in *The Strange Islands* Merton dealt more critically with religious themes. In place of the earlier bliss he included poems that considered ugly aspects of religious life, as in "To a Severe Nun," "Whether There is Enjoyment in Bitterness," and "Birdcage Walk." In "Whether There is Enjoyment in Bitterness" he reflects wryly on some confining aspects of the life he had got himself into, the life of a professionally good man: "Am I not/ Permitted (like other men)/To be sick of myself?" (*CP*, p. 231). Similarly, in "Birdcage Walk," one of the better poems in *The Strange Islands*, authoritarianism in the religious life is condemned in the figure of the "gaitered bishop" whose insular, privileged existence excludes him from contact with the "paradise bird" (*CP*, pp. 275-276).

There are positive poems, however, and a few of these, like

"Elegy for the Monastery Barn" and "Elias — Variations on a Theme," are exceptionally fine. "Elegy for the Monastery Barn" was written following an interrupted evening meditation in August 1953 when the old monastery cowbarn burned down: "The monks left the meditation to fight a very hot fire and the poem arrived about the same time as the fire truck from the nearest town."[30] The incident recalled a childhood experience that had left Merton with an impression of burning barns as "great mysteries."[31] The poem's success derives in part from its complex tone. The tone is sympathetic yet satiric, warm yet urbane, tender yet witty. The wit of the poem lies in the vision of the ancient, flaming barn as a grand old dowager overtaken suddenly by a completely uninhibited mood:

As though an aged person were to wear
Too gay a dress
And walk about the neighborhood
Announcing the hour of her death. (CP, p. 288)

The poem is anchored serenely in a "summer day's end,/ At suppertime, when wheels are still," the scene matching the dignity and placidness of the dying lady, who "stands apart" and "will not have us near her" (CP, p. 288). Death on this occasion comes discreetly and when expected ("The long, hushed gallery/ Clean and resigned and waiting for the fire"). Thrown up by the blaze are images of the barn's past, including fifty "invisible" cattle that in the conflagration have found their "destiny" and their "meaning" (CP, p. 289). The tone changes imperceptibly from being courtly and whimiscal to apocalyptic. The poem's conclusion focuses on the final meaning of the fire: "Let no man stay inside to look upon the Lord!" Harnessed throughout by a carefully modulated tone, the poem carries its message of epiphany with quiet and assured eloquence.

"Elias — Variations on a Theme" shows Merton experimenting with the short line and with polyphonic structure. The careful knitting of images and lines is impressive and creates a climate of concentration that is almost narcotic. Merton had always iden-tified with the "burnt faces" of the prophets, seeing them as

transformed and made great by the "white-hot dangerous presence of inspiration."[32] He focuses in the poem on the period of
Elias's life when the prophet had been "felled by despair under
the juniper tree" while trying to find his way to Mount Horeb
and God.[33] The juniper becomes a "blunt pine," which along
with the motifs of the fire and the bird, serves as the basis of the
fugal arrangement:

> Under the blunt pine
> In the winter sun
> The pathway dies
> And the wilds begin.
> Here the bird abides
> Where the ground is warm. (CP, pp. 239-240)

The pattern of sound is divided between muffled and high-
pitched vowels. This division parallels the contrast between the
rooted pine and the bird, which like the soul of the prophet
wants to rise. The pattern is repeated in variations throughout
the poem.

Elias's fiery chariot is compared in alternating images to one of
the abbey's farm wagons:

> This old wagon
> With the wet, smashed wheels
> Is better. ("My chariot")
> This derelict is better.
> ("Of fire.") (CP, pp. 241-242)

Merton's homely wagon is suitable for his spiritual growth because it is unlike the fiery chariots of technocracy ("Grand machines, all flame,/ With supernatural wings") and instead resembles nature, which in its dilapidated state it will soon rejoin:

> Better still the old trailer ("My chariot")
> With the dead stove in it, and the rain
> Comes down the pipe and covers the floor. Bring me
> My old chariot of broken-down rain. (CP, p. 242)

Like the bird and the ascending fire Merton's rain-soaked, rustic chariot speeds "faster and faster" as it "stands still." Faster and faster it "stays where it has always been" (CP, p. 242). The poem thus reaches the still point of Merton's turning world.

Included in *The Strange Islands* is a verse play, "The Tower of Babel," which Merton wrote as a modern morality play but which might more properly be called a dramatic poem. The tower symbolizes the hubris of technology as well as the abuse of language that he regarded as inevitable in a culture in which communication was primarily mechanical. Language becomes an "instrument of war. Words of the clocks and devils. Words of the wheels and machines. Steel words stronger than flesh or spirit. Secret words which divide the essences of things" (CP, p. 252). "The Tower of Babel" is divided into two major segments, the rise and fall of the tower and the restoration of the world on a village level and in harmony with nature. The characters are somewhat wooden, being spokesmen for various points of view. There is little interaction between them. The work is modestly successful and there are moments of fine poetry, as in the image of the divine cloud that comes up "out of the desert no bigger than a man's fist," hovering over the tower like a "man's arm" and expanding steadily until "suddenly the burly dark filled the whole sky" (CP, pp. 252-253).

Merton's next volume, *Emblems of a Season of Fury* (1963), appeared in the midst of his strenuous social writing. He thought the book an odd collection of things. Among its heterogeneous materials it contains translations of Latin American poets and some poetic prose. Among the poems are monologues in which Merton assumes the identity of a historical character, such as in "News from the School at Chartres" and "What to Think when it Rains Blood." The prosody shows a steady loosening and expansion in the lines and stanzas as well as a greater colloquialism than ever. With punctuation almost nonexistent the lines flow freely. In terms of subject matter the collection is divided into poems of social protest and Zen poems.

The shift to social protest was stimulated by Merton's sense that civilized values had vanished. In the "Elegy for James Thurber," he wrote bluntly: "Business and generals survive you."[34] Some of the protest poems, like "A Picture of Lee Ying" and the "Chant to be Used in Processions around a Site with Furnaces," are restrained and understated. The "Chant" was particularly effective. The speaker's reasonable and accommodating manner made him an apt symbol for Merton not only of the horrors of Nazi Germany but also, analogously, of the new race generated by technocracy. The emphasis on cleanliness in the Nazi ovens struck Merton as a symbol of the technologist's antipathy to messiness.

Much of the imagery in *Emblems of a Season of Fury* is made to flare — as in "The Moslems' Angel of Death," which is about the Algerian war of independence in the early 1960s. Death appears as a great honeycomb of bees with "million fueled eyes" (*CP*, p. 307). At the conclusion of death's visit there are only embers, "one red coal left burning/ Beneath the ashes of the great vision" and one "blood-red eye left open/ When the city is burnt out" (*CP*, p. 308). The poems seethe with urgency and discontent. Even the Greek myths, which were generally used as symbols of order in a chaotic world, seem hard-pressed to contain their volatile subjects, as in "Gloss on the Sin of Ixion." Ixion's fathering of the monstrous race of Centaurs, accomplished by a bizarre, onanistic union with a cloud, is used by Merton as a symbol of the rape of the world by greed and technology. The giant "mechanical boys" that issue from this rape are paralleled by the "spill" of sun and planets and the ravishing of "sacred man" (*CP*, p. 314).

The heat of Merton's burning world is so intense that it consumes prophets as well as those who are responsible for the flames. In "Advice to a Young Prophet" he focuses on "private lunatics" like the hippies as well as on those beat poets like Ginsberg who took to "mescaline" and who retreated to the "unlucky mountain" to dance and "shake the sin/ Out of their feet and hands" (*CP*, p. 338). Merton felt that even if they failed to free themselves from personal frailties these afflicted visionaries did not at least, as others had done, contribute to the destruction of society. In addition they were the heirs of a pure and noble tradition:

America needs these fatal friends
Of God and country to grovel in mystical ashes,
Pretty big prophets whose words don't burn,
Fighting the strenuous imago all day long. (CP, p. 339)

Merton's courage is shown in the way he directed his anger against some respected American achievements. In "Why Some Look Up to Planets and Heroes" he characterized the American astronaut as "Brooding and seated at the summit/ Of a well-engineered explosion" — a "tourist" flung into the "public" sky by an "ingenious weapon/Prepared for every legend" (CP, p. 305). He described the astronauts as rocketing into a space that had already been violated by "apes and Russians." He was sensitive about the poem's effect, but he felt that although space exploration represented a stunning display of intelligence and bravery, his poem had not addressed itself to this aspect, but rather to the diversion from man's critical needs brought about by the space extravaganza. He had asked in Wisdom in the Desert: "What can we gain by sailing to the moon if we are not able to cross the abyss that separates us from ourselves. This is the most important of all voyages of discovery, and without it all the rest are not only useless but disastrous."[35] In like vein he wrote to a friend in 1968 that although he could get excited over space travel as a sort of cosmic and ritual shamanic dance," he was repelled by the chauvinism, the commercialism, the "hubris and cliché" that surrounded the whole business.[36] He sensed space as the last frontier and as a contemplative resented the intrusion of technological man into it, characterizing space flight as the "last apocalyptic myth of machinery propagating its own kind in the eschatological wilderness of space."[37]

He did not offer particular solutions to what was going on, telling a friend in 1967 that he was "just hanging out the wash and letting it fly in the breeze."[38] He was prepared to offer a general alternative to the behavior of contemporary man, however, and he tried to illustrate this alternative in some of the Zen lyrics included in Emblems of a Season of Fury. "O Sweet Irrational Worship" is an example:

Wind and a bobwhite
And the afternoon sun.

By ceasing to question the sun
I have become light,

Bird and wind.
My leaves sing.
I am earth, earth
All these lighted things
Grow from my heart. (*CP*, p. 344)

The earth song conveys Merton's consciousness of the ground of being, a basis upon which men could share their experience when they otherwise seemed consumed by their differences. "Song for Nobody " "Love Winter When the Plant Says Nothing," "The Fall," "Grace's House," and "Night-Flowering Cactus" express the Edenic note in Merton's consciousness, the note that balances the apocalyptic aspects of his vision. In connection with "Grace's House," a poem that dealt with his ecstatic response to a child's drawing, he exclaims that we "do not know where we are" and sets forth his paradisal vision as at least as genuine as the pessimism and "folly" of those who see only the "imago, the absurd spectre, the mask over our own emptiness."[39]

"Love Winter When the Plant Says Nothing" focuses on the life that lies hidden within the dormant plant, a life that is analogous to the paradisal spark that Merton saw in all men—the "burly infant spot," the "golden zero" (*CP*, p. 353). The poem is grounded in the action of nature, and the meanings are not insistent and in fact are not even articulated, but instead are latent within the details of the scene — evidence of Merton's growing poetic command. The direction of his work from this point is toward objectivity, simplicity, and firmness.

The years between *Emblems of a Season of Fury* and *Cables to the Ace* were filled with change. Settled into his hermitage, Merton was in the process of winding down his prose writing and concentrating on more creative writing, particularly poetry. As part of this ferment he launched a poetry journal, *Monk's Pond*. He liked the experience of editing and valued the contacts that he made with other, particularly younger, poets. As well as poems by these younger writers, he ran poems by Kerouac, Zukofsky, and Wendell Berry in addition to some of his own work, including an early draft of a section from *The Geography of Lograire* and some concrete poems.

During this period he published poems in a number of journals, many of them on social themes —like the "Letters to Che," "Picture of a Black Child with a white Doll," "Secular Signs," and "For the Spanish Poet Miguel Hernandez." In the latter poem he summarized the role of the poet in troubled times:

> When the light spine of a society
> Bends and crackles
> There is needed space and sense
> For some peculiar spark
> In the free tenements.[40]

Because of his ill health Merton was forced into an ironic acknowledgement of his reliance upon technology. He had had a piece of metal surgically inserted near his cervical disc. The incident provides the underlying irony for the poem "With the World in My Bloodstream" that was published in 1967. In the hospital the metal insertion gives him an ironic feeling of affinity with the society he had left, and he characterizes himself as growing "hungry for invented air/ And for the technical community of men."[41] The experience causes him to recall his earlier life in the world and to feel a sudden and whimsical attachment to "the unmarried fancy/ And the wild gift I made in those days." The bold colloquialism of Merton's later style is conveyed through the question that hangs over the poem: "I wonder who the hell I am" (*CP*, p. 615).

His notebooks at this time are filled with poems and poetic fragments that reveal the new direction in which his mind was moving and the new freedom that was conferred by his hermit life. One of these poems, "I Always Obey My Nurse," written in 1966 but unpublished as yet, shows him in a state of conflict with himself:

I always obey my nurse
I always take care
of my bleeding sin
My fractured religion.[42]

The love poem, though platonic, exposed Merton's dilemma
with respect to his future. Although the experience undermined
his feeling of integrity as a religious man, it had the unexpected
effect of strengthening some of his deepest beliefs, as can be seen
in the concluding refrain: "And God did not make death!"

This ferment brought about a revolution in his style and in his
themes, as is apparent in his last poems, Cables to the Ace and The
Geography of Lograire. Merton called Cables to the Ace (1968) an
"antipoem" and indicated in his prologue to that work that it
would be a poem without much of an emphasis on imagery,
sound, and rhythm. Instead, he offered parodies of Wordsworth
and Coleridge, whose themes and poetics, he argued, were no
longer an appropriate idiom for contemporary verse. He insisted
that poets must recognize that the experience of most people was
unpoetic and that the poet's function was to sift through the
clutter that people had in their minds in order to see what could
be made of it artistically:

> The antipoet "suggests" a tertiary meaning which is not
> creative and "original" but a deliberate ironic feedback
> of cliché, a further referential meaning, alluding, by its
> tone, banality, etc., to a customary and abused context,
> that of an impoverished and routine sensibility, and of
> the "mass-mind," the stereotyped creation of quantita-
> tive preordained response by "mass-culture."[43]

The ironic feedback would, he assumed, jolt the reader into a
consciousness of his stereotypic lifestyle.

His new poetic voice would be "racy, insolent, direct, profane,
iconoclastic, and earthy," a hip language that would even have
its own "magic incantation and myth," thereby paralleling the

"ponderous and self-important utterances" of the establishment. It would, however, be more concrete than establishment
jargon, more in contact with "relevant experience," the hard
realities of "poverty, brutality, vice, and resistance."[44]
    The antipoem was part of Merton's campaign against the de-
basement of language by social institutions and the media, a
corrosion of the communal sensibility that substituted
stereotypes for responses that should have been personal and
immediate. His antidote was the encouragement of spontaneous
utterance. If the free flow of language sometimes resulted in
awkwardness, it also released the face that was "sweating under
the mask."[45] He believed that this spontaneous outflow would
allow the poet to accumulate fresh experience and an original
idiom, both of which could then be shaped into disciplined,
innovative expression.
    The stimulus to write antipoetry came principally from Mer-
ton's contact with the Chilean poet Nicanor Parra, some of whose
Poems and Antipoems were translated by him in 1967. Parra's style
was flat, understated, and relaxed, eschewing any hint of lyricism or symbolism.[46] He was fascinated by the dry, disconcerting voice of Parra, and he took to heart Parra's liberating advice
to the poets of the world:

> Write as you will
> In whatever style you like
> Too much blood has run under the bridge
> To go on believing
> That only one road is right.
>
> In poetry everything is permitted.[47]

    In writing *Cables to the Ace* Merton was also influenced by Bob
Dylan, whose iconoclastic songs seemed to him to have the sort
of saltiness he wanted. Herbert Marcuse also affected him at this
time, having demonstrated how mass culture tended to be "an-
ticulture," stifling creative work by the "sheer volume of what is
'produced,' or reproduced." Given this situation, Merton felt
that the poet no longer had to parody; it was enough to quote.[48]
Marshall McLuhan, the oracle of the media and of the electronic

age was also an obvious influence, as can be seen in these lines:

> Some say that the electric world
> Is a suspicious village
> Or better a jungle where all the howls
> Are banal.[49]

Merton went further than McLuhan in relating the glut of public discourse to the alienation of contemporary man, whom he portrayed as traveling alone in a "small blue capsule of indignation" (*CP*, p. 397). While McLuhan visualized the electronic world as one of process, without beginning, end, or meaning, Merton found himself balking at this sort of analysis. Realizing that many observers, theologians among them, could not wait to restructure their world views along McLuhanesque lines, he drew back:

> Afflicted as I am with an incurable case of metaphysics, I cannot see where the idea of Godhead as process is more dynamic than that of Godhead as *pure act*. To one who has been exposed to scholastic ontology and has not recovered, it remains evident that the activity *of becoming* is considerably less alive and dynamic than the *act of Being*.[50]

As well as inserting a parody of a newscast into *Cables to the Ace*, Merton dropped a number of advertisements into the sequence as part of his portrait of the ephemeral but hypnotic surface of American experience:

> I will get up and go to Marble country
> Where deadly smokes grow out of moderate heat
> And all the cowboys look for fortunate slogans
> Among horses' asses. (*CP*, p. 434)

He wrote to friends like W. H. Ferry asking for "good, gaudy, noisy *ad* material."[51] Ferry sent him a load of stuff, and Merton wrote back begging him to shut off the tap:

for petesake no tearsheets from Playboy. I am very grateful to you for the advertising material I needed, which came in the form of Fortune, etc. But enough! It was all I could take. Am still retching. Weak stomach. Getting old. Too long in the woods. Can't handle Esq. Old gut won't hold it.[52]

He was aware that the ephemeral nature of these materials could undermine the integrity of his poetry, but he wrote to a friend in 1968 that he felt *Cables* still represented a right approach, even if "dour" and "perhaps shallow."[53]

Merton designed *Cables to the Ace* as a mosaic of prose and poetry. The effect of the mosaic structure, he explained in a letter to poet Robert Lax, was to create the atmosphere in which the parts of the poem were suspended in "mid air between true and false, between the Island of Staten and the Island of Coney, an everlasting pons asinorum."[54] He had thus brought his work into line with the collage technique used by a number of his contemporaries, although his tonelessness and antipoetic approach are somewhat unusual. He referred to the sections of *Cables to the Ace* as cantos and tried to create the impression of a poem that could be read "forwards or backwards," as he put it in a letter to James Laughlin.[55] Unlike a chronological pattern, the mosaic arrangement allowed the reader to be simultaneously conscious of all of the parts of the poem, thereby remaining alert in any one section to the overall design. This structuring encouraged a meditative reading of the poem since there was no pressure to get to the end in order to see the meaning of the work unfold.

A unifying force in the book is the motif of cables themselves, which in spite of Merton's intention to adopt a somewhat literal style, clearly symbolize the connectedness of the poem's various subjects. This connectedness is revealed through a series of metaphorical analogies. At a surface level the title alludes to messages sent, as well as to the electronic wizardry that revolutionized modern communications. Merton's cables are physical structures — electronic wiring used in telephones and the media, as well as cables suspending bridges that connect cities. Bridge cables are analogously likened in turn to other advances in transportation and communication, like the "long jets" whose trajectories "string their hungry harps/ Across the storm" (*CP*, p. 425).

Through Merton's free-flowing associative pattern the vibrations of various kinds of steel wires are juxtaposed, from the metallic sound of electric guitars to the sibilance of the Aeolian harp with which the guitars are polarized. The steel guitars lead symbolically to the steel cables of technology which could be made musical, Merton notes dryly, if played by "full-armed societies doomed to an electric war" (*CP*, p. 396). The presence of the cable motif is so pervasive that even people are depicted as cables, a metamorphosis that eventually overtakes even the narrator:

> . . . an entire sensate parcel
> Of registered earth
> Working my way through adolescence
> To swim dashing storms
> Of amusement and attend
> The copyrighted tornado
> Of sheer sound. (*CP*, p. 447)

Merton is approached along the cable that leads to him, the "long road of winding steel," by people with "modest anxieties" who seek him out in the "beautiful cellars" in which the poet lives out his nocturnal and unhallowed existence (*CP*, pp. 431-432).

The sequence of poems is divided into three principal thematic worlds, and the tension between these worlds is what gives the poem its dramatic interest. The first is a McLuhanesque world of process, which is epitomized in the line that announces that cables "are never causes. Noises are never values" (*CP*, p. 396). Those who inhabited the world of process, Merton believed, were the duped majority who had been manipulated by the corrupt charms of advertising and the media:

Top pliable males
Who have always been boys at heart
Drag-racing through darkest Esquire.
Ready to become style leaders
And medium shapes. (CP, p. 406)

The hedonistic and stylish progress of contemporary man
through the maze of cables is portrayed in the belittling terms of
insect servility:

Each ant has his appointed round
In the technical circuit
All the way to high
One to make it and the other to break it. (CP, p. 430)

The insect metaphor recalls the section of the poem in which rats
supervise the laboratory experiments in which men are run
through an electronic maze. The rats, who manipulate society's
mythdreams, keep those in the maze passive and satisfied by
pressing pleasure buttons:

That earthly
Paradise in the head
Two millimeters away
From my sinus infection. (CP, p. 409)

Merton's brave new world centers on a society that values
nothing but pleasure and that therefore methodically attempts to
suppress feelings of guilt and alienation:

Now the psycho —
Electric jump
Into spasm:

A ticking spark

Feels great
Kills the snakes
And the odor of heresy. (*CP*, p. 416)

Cables focuses on a world that strives toward sensuality, but finds natural and spontaneous physical pleasure is no longer possible. Merton was appalled by the antiseptic format that advertising gave to love so that even lust was no longer animal; it was chemical and electric. Following the lead of the advertisements, his lovers ensure that: "We are not overheated, we smell good and we remain smooth. No skin needs to be absolutely private for all are quiet, clean, and cool" (*CP*, p. 422). Privacy has been stripped away and men and women are manipulated through the scenarios of love suggested by the media into a synthetic, dissonant sexuality:

Determined to love
Lured by the barbarous fowl
He enters the rusty thicket of wires
Where nothing is tame

He meets his artiste
Who invites him to her ballet
There the swimming head
Makes everybody bleed.

Hanging on the wires
Love is still warm. (*CP*, p. 443)

The frankness of the language is a measure of how far Merton had come since his first modest lyrics.

A second thematic world in *Cables to the Ace* is that inhabited by the administrators of contemporary society. They are depicted as an elite minority of unusually purposeful people:

Political man must learn
To work his pleasure button
And cut off the controlling rat
Science is very near but the morbid
Animal might always win. (CP, p. 409)

The politicians, who thrive on power instead of pleasure, are paralleled by the generals, who resemble the machines they model themselves after, taking care to maintain themselves in "good condition" (CP, p. 417). The generals dispatch bomber pilots to kill with utter detachment, looking through lenses that "discover blue flame/ In the mouths/ Of fatal children" (CP, p. 405). The pervasiveness of the motif of manipulation is typical of the way in which Cables to the Ace manifests a convincing unity beneath its casual arrangement of surface detail.

The administrators in Merton's pleasure dome are portrayed as sharks:

Cutlash Finn
To kill time
Before and aft —
Er he sinks his fin
Again in his
Own wake. (CP, p. 410)

The passage depicts the shark as both predator and victim, a sign of Merton's perception that self-defeat was implicit in the way in which contemporary society was managed. The ironic defeat of the manipulators by themselves reaches apocalyptic proportions by the end of the book:

The flash of falling metals. The shower of parts, cameras, guns of experience in the waste heaven of deadly rays. Cataclysm of designs. Out of the meteor sky cascades the efficient rage of our team. Down comes another blazing and dissolute unit melting in mid-air over a fortunate suburb. A perishing computer blazes down into a figure of fire and steam. We live under the rain of stainless leaders.(*CP*, pp. 452-453)

Merton depicts the administrators of technocracy as maintaining their power by being able to provide ready institutionalized responses to personal anxieties:

For a nominal fee one can confide in a cryphone
With sobs of champagne
Or return from sudden sport to address
The monogag
The telefake
The base undertones of the confessional speaker
Advising trainees
Through cloistered earphones. (*CP*, p. 418)

The chief symbol for the victimization of modern man through the manipulation of language is Caliban, whose brutal face hovers over the poems. Contemporary man looks back patronizingly at his atavistic ancestors because of their ignorance of language — "He walked on two syllables/ Or maybe none" (*CP*, p. 399). However, he is viewed as in some respects in a worse position than primitive man, manipulated semantically by technocrats and unconsoled by academics, who are able only to "mime the arts of diction" instead of revitalizing the language (*CP*, p. 405).

Poets are able to counteract the debasement of language, but theirs is an underground existence. The poet's cables to the world are therefore coded, as indeed is Merton's sequence of poems, gibberish to conventional minds, but meaningful to those who are alert and pure of heart. An example of such a coded poetic message is the poem "The Prospects of Nostradamus," in which a terrifying outcome for the world is predicted:

Day of the grunt
The incision
The killer rat
Two-thousand
Year of the low tone . . .
The bluebottle
Two-thousand
Year of the white bone. (CP, pp. 439-440)

The passage summarizes central motifs — the grunt of inarticu-
late man and the killer rat. These motifs are linked with a
culminating vision of death — the white bone and the carrion-
feeding bluebottle fly — in a synoptic vision that establishes the
role of the poet as seer.

The problem faced by the poet is: what is the point in his being
able to see clearly when the contemporary world has nothing in it
that is worth seeing? In this situation the poet is reduced to
peripheral and obsolete work, interpreting the "ministry of the
stars" and the "broken gear of a bird." He is left to test the quality
of stone lights, "ashen fruits of a fire's forgotten service," and his
sayings, like those of the saint, are "put away in air-conditioned
archives" (CP, p. 396).

On the artist's side is the discontent within the hearts of those
who are herded about in society, a discontent that runs deeper
than the cloying sensuality with which their lives are filled:

. . . lowdown
At the bottom of deep water
Deeper than Anna Livia Plurabelle
Or any other river
Some nameless rebel
A Mister Houdini or somebody with fingers
Slips the technical knots
Pops the bubbles in the head
Runs the vote backwards
And turns the bloody cooler
All the way
OFF. (CP, p. 436)

The "cooler" is the air-conditioned nightmare. Switching off the thermostat is the first step in an inner revolution that involves an affirmation of the self that will eventually revolutionize society.

The man within is represented by a primitive, almost prenatal speech that is depicted as emerging from the unconscious:

> What do you teach me
> Mama my cow?
> (My delicate forefathers
> Wink in their sleep)
> What do you seek of me
> Mama my ocean. (CP, pp. 400-401)

The voice of the unconscious would eventually challenge the suffocation of the self by its environment and reestablish its bond with nature and with its deepest sources — "Mama my ocean."

Another thematic world in *Cables to the Ace* is that of nature and God, the "ace" of Merton's title. Technology is polarized with God and nature as a sort of antipoem, a burlesque of the life force — as is seen in "The Planet Over Eastern Parkway," one of the better poems in the sequence:

> And the cart wheel planet
> Goes down in the silos of earth
> Whose parkways vanish in the steam
> Of ocean feeling
> Or the houses of oil-men. (CP, p. 401)

Pitting himself against the exploitation of the planet and reaffirming his belief in natural connections, Merton describes his own "center" as being in the "teeming heart of natural families" (CP, p. 443).

If man's speech had been vulgarized beyond repair, there was always the subtler speech of being itself with which to refresh the spirit:

Warm sun. Perhaps these yellow wild-flowers have the minds of little girls. My worship is a blue sky and ten thousand crickets in the deep wet hay of the field. My vow is the silence under their song. I admire the woodpecker and the dove in simple mathematics of flight. Together we study practical norms. The plowed and planted field is red as a brick in the sun and says: *"Now my turn!"* Several of us begin to sing. (*CP*, p. 400)

Natural and mystical values are asserted late in the poem, and the concluding pieces open up the rich geography of Merton's interior world, supplanting the discord of the earlier poems. The final notes played on the cable's harp are those of the natural harmony and fecundity that offset the sterility of the contemporary world, as can be seen in "The Harmonies of Excess":

The hidden lovers in the soil
Become green plants and gardens tomorrow
When they are ordered to re-appear
In the wet sun's poem
Then they force the delighted
Power of buds to laugh louder
They scatter all the cries of light
Like shadow rain and make their bed
Over and over in the hollow flower
The violet bonfire. (*CP*, pp. 447-448)

The sequence builds surely and evocatively toward its epiphany, having shrugged off its prosaic and ironic language:

Slowly slowly
Comes Christ through the garden
Speaking to the sacred trees
Their branches bear his light
Without harm. (*CP*, p. 449)

Astrological symbols herald the return of the perception of natural order as the poem moves away from the depiction of the whole society and toward the isolated vision of the narrator. In addition to the cosmic harmony to which the narrator is sensitive, there is the suggestion of a world that has both purpose and process.

The movement of *Cables to the Ace* shifts toward the end from being unfocused and ironic, a scatter-gun effect, to the concentrated lyrical pursuit of the destination of all cables— "Infinite Zero," the "ace of freedoms" (*CP*, pp. 452, 454). In the cybernetic wasteland of contemporary society the narrator proclaims his irrelevancy with the final image of the birds, which, without any apparent control, fly "uncorrected across burnt lands." As opposed to the sophisticated expectations of the electronic age Merton concludes that we learn in fact "by the cables of orioles" (*CP*, p. 454). The image consummates his overall design, making *Cables to the Ace* something of a technical *tour de force* in spite of the ostensibly unpoetic nature of some of its materials.

The Geography of Lograire (1969) was greeted with respectful nods by critics, one of them calling it the "year's most important book of poems."[56] Merton had begun the work in 1967, writing to his publisher, James Laughlin, that he had started on yet another poetic sequence that would again be "far out."[57] He wrote to W. H. Ferry in the same year that he thought the new poetic sequence would develop into something quite lively and complex, calling it his "summa of offbeat anthropology."[58] He told yet another friend that the poem, a "big poetic mosaic," had originally centered around his interest in the cargo religious movements of the South Pacific.[59]

Merton regarded *The Geography of Lograire* as a "purely tentative first draft of a longer work in progress," what he referred to as the "first opening up of the dream."[60] Sister Thérèse Lentfoehr in a note appended to *The Geography of Lograire* has written that the name "Lograire" was derived from the real name of Francois Villon (Francois Des Loges) as well as from a type of cabin used by French foresters, an obvious connection with Merton's wooded hermitage (*CP*, pp. 596-597). Whatever the exact referents of Merton's title were, he launched himself ambitiously with *The Geography of Lograire* as a poet of psychogeography. He arranged his sequence into a loose alternation of prose and poetry, encompassing the experience of man's history as well as his own. Furthermore, he grounded the poems vividly in particular locales, something that he had not always done in earlier poems.

Among the alternating passages of prose and poetry Merton included raw quotations from his readings in history and anthropology along with other extracts that had evidently been filtered through his sensibility. His notebook for *The Geography of Lograire* is filled with quotations and thumbnail sketches of historical people. He was impressed with the imaginative, non-chronological arrangement of parts of the Old Testament which he felt gave a truer picture of history than could be achieved by using a factual and linear approach. He compared his conception of history to the structure of a song. In a song one did not think of the beginning of the melody as lost in the past but as still present at the end. History too was such a unified whole, held suspended as such in the "consciousness of a unified people."[61]

Thus, critics who reacted against the surface fragmentation of *The Geography of Lograire* missed the point of what Merton was trying to do. The multitude of allusions and shifting viewpoints achieves unity on a thematic level, especially in terms of his cyclical conception of history. In addition, as in *Cables to the Ace*, the poems are bound together through the unifying vision of the narrator, who serves as the hub of both the outer and inner geographical exploration in the poem: "*Geography./ I am all (here)/ There!*" (*CP*, p. 498).

The use of the motif of geography to plot the course of history was a skillful move on Merton's part and helped to secure the poem's immediacy. We think of geography as in the present and of history as in the past. Merton's excursions into geographical zones allowed him to move not only outward but back in time since he made a point of visiting primitive societies. He concentrated on cultural configurations that for him, sometimes for him alone, represented significant points in the development of man.

One of the important metaphors in *The Geography of Lograire* is the parallax. The poem is multi-dimensional, even cubistic, in dramatizing with complex simultaneity both the flux of civilization and the isolated and critical sensibility of the narrator. This complexity is enhanced by Merton's skill in varying the tone, pace, texture, and density of the various poems in the sequence. The underlying tone is one of restraint and concerned objectivity. He wanted to keep clear of the commentary that had been part of some of his earlier poetry, and he concentrated instead on what he called an "urbane structuralism" (*CP*, p. 458).

His method of mixing cultural anomalies like the Sioux ghost dances and the cargo cults with his own experience as a contemporary man had the effect of integrating these anomalies into the stream of contemporary thought so that their relevance could be appreciated. It must be remembered that for Merton the secrets of healthy civilization had been lost beneath the withering impact of industrialism, and while some of his examples of culture with their accompanying mythdreams were bizarre and obscure, he felt nonetheless that all could yield insights into the human condition, and he tried to demonstrate this in his portrayal of the cultural shock that overtook not only primitive but modern man.

The intricately designed prologue to *The Geography of Lograire* introduces most of the principal themes, including the Cain/Abel motif, the symbol of the funnel house, and the figure of Ulysses — in addition to motifs from Merton's personal history and geography. The effect of the yoking of different cultures and periods is to illuminate the fundamental similarities among them, thereby giving the reader a poignant sense of lost opportunities for unity among peoples of the world. The prologue opens with allusions to Wales and England ("pale eyed Albion"), Germany, and finally America, the sources of Merton's own history and geography. His genetic and historical descent is traced against the background of the wood thrush's song, a sign of the embrace of history by nature.

He tried to free language from conventional syntax in order to find a new idiom for his mythdream and in order to restore the kind of vitality to language that he was certain it had lost:

Should Wales dark Wales slow ways sea coal tar
Green tar sea stronghold is Wales my grand
Dark my Wales land father it was green
With all harps played over and bells. (*CP*, p. 459)

The distribution of the parts of speech in the passage, as if they were blocks in a game of Scrabble, has the effect of breaking up the reader's preconceptions about what is to follow in each of the lines. He frustrates the kind of reader who wants to quickly put the pieces together. Nevertheless, the pieces do fit. Wales is pictured as dark in that it is linked with the hardships of sea voyages of the past, with slavery (the Tarhead Captain), and with the slag heaps that mar the Welsh landscape. For Merton, Wales represented the raw and primitive yet richly mysterious matrix of the past. He plays with the images of "land" and "grand" father in order to focus on the earthiness of his past, including its connection with a fertile, unpredictable nature, a nature that in turn traced its origins back to the sea. The harps obviously symbolize the Celtic culture from which Merton stemmed and to which he always felt close.

In addition, the prologue simultaneously sketches the development of Western Europe and the subsequent discovery of the new world, a montage effect that adds greatly to the depth and power of the sequence. The Cain/Abel motif is implicit in the story of the old world sea captains, but it becomes intensified in the depiction of the new world, a world that is eventually scarred by the mortal fall of the Civil War:

Pain and Abel lay down red designs
Civil is slain brother sacred wall wood pine
Sacred black brother is beaten to the wall. (CP, pp. 461-462)

Blacks are portrayed as bringing their culture to an America that neither wants nor recognizes its value: "Dahomey pine tar small wood bench bucket/ There coil ire design father of Africa pattern" (CP, p. 462). The result is that the transplanted black slaves are subjected to severe cultural shock — prefiguring one of the poem's principal themes.

The funnel motif, which is linked to Merton's reading of Dante, is introduced within the funereal context of the 'dies irae' and thus foreshadows the most surrealistic and apocalyptic section of the poem — "Queens Tunnel." The figure of Ulysses, the heroic quester, parallels the narrator's wandering and links the poem not only with historical peoples but with epic worlds spun by the imaginations of great writers.

The poem proper begins with "South," because that is where Merton is, and he is the center of the geography of Lograire. The American South is dramatized against the background of Kentucky and Florida. The dominant motif of the Civil War which figures in the prologue is narrowed here to fit the Kentucky landscape. The canto opens with a brief look at the Cain/Abel motif, which anticipates the section's racial theme. Merton focuses first, though, on the bridge over the Ohio river at Louisville ("rivercity") that is travelled by soldiers from Fort Knox in search of women. The atmosphere recalls the electronic jungle in *Cables to the Ace*, a depraved world of sex, drugs, and blaring horns. The poem races by turnpike from one section of Kentucky to another against a background of "neo-strange" music and "lighted copperheads" (*CP*, p. 470), an allusion to Kentucky's historical role as a border state. The acceleration of modern life, which has finally strangled Kentucky, as it has every other part of America, is set against the more traditional violence of the feuding hill people and the racism of the Ku Klux Klan, the Southern Cains. The bedrock of Southern religiosity is represented ironically in the description of these people as "Paschal" Cains, which also symbolizes the innocence of the maltreated blacks who, being likened to the sacrificial lamb, are the key to the salvation of the whites: "Maybe he has two manors one for Sundays/ One for weeks anger kicked out nigger" (CP, pp. 466-467). The pun on "manors" brings into the poem a picture of the fine old Georgian plantation houses that were the backbone both of Southern gentility and of slavery.

"Miami You Are about to be Surprised" focuses on the Hiltonism of a southern pleasure city. The languid atmosphere of the setting is offset by a stern tone of foreboding, the resulting tension forming the basis of Merton's design for the poem:

> You are going to be warned
> By a gourmet with a mouthful of seaweed
> Reaching all the way through superb
> Armholes. (*CP*, p. 474)

The hedonistic primitiveness of Miami is contrasted with the genuine and fruitful primitiveness of the "Thonga Lament," which describes a deep African mythdream.

"Notes for a New Liturgy" follows, depicting the anthropomorphic projection of a black God by an African prophet who is resourceful enough to launch his own religion. While comic and outlandish, the dreamed Church is seen as at least a mark above the mass-produced mythdreams of a lobotomized Western society. As part of Merton's portrayal of one culture's adaptation to another, the African prophet unconsciously parodies the most stultifying aspects of missionary Christianity, describing himself as a "Prime-Mover in Management" and conducting his liturgy in a way that amounts to a macabre admixture of native shamanism and eucharistic ritual:

"HOLD THIS MITRE WHILE I STRANGLE
CHICKENS AND THROW THEM IN THE AIR
COVERING THE SACRED STONE WITH BLOODY
FEATHERS." (CP, p. 479)

The macabre humor adds an important dimension to *The Geography of Lograire*, and as it is unaccompanied by any trace of Merton's earlier querulousness, the effect is to keep the poems urbane and tight.

From Africa the poem moves to Latin America, which for Merton was always a powerful opposing symbol to the decadence and sterility of North America. He deals particularly with the Mayan culture, which he regarded as one of the noblest and most peaceful in history. Here Merton quotes and condenses sections of Maud Makemson's *Book of the Jaguar Priest*, a translation of the *Book of Chilam Balam of Tizimin* (1951), which gave the Mayan version of the Spanish conquest of America.

The section begins optimistically with a poem about Xochipilli, the flower giver, and the benign rituals that were associated with him:

Some ate no chili others at midnight
Took their corn soup with a flower

Floating in the middle.
They call this the "Fast of Flowers."

Month nine: in fields and patches
Of corn gather flowers
Bring them in armfuls
To the feasting house
Keep them overnight
Then at dawn
Make thick garlands
For the god's yard and day. (*CP*, pp. 480-481)

The graceful, ritual dancing of the men and women that follows is punctuated by an ironic echo from the journals of the Spanish missionaries, who had failed to see the beauty of the Mayan rituals: "Such were the services which their demons commanded them" (*CP*, p. 482).

Precolonial Mayan culture was for Merton a symbol of the paradise that is possible for all:

The ladies of Tlatilco
Wore nothing but turbans
(Skirts only for a dance)
A lock of hair over the eyes
Held only by a garland
Tassels and leaves
They bleached their black hair
With lime
Like the Melanesians. (*CP*, p. 484)

Though it does not disrupt the mood of pastoral innocence, the description of the women bleaching their hair is an ironic foreshadowing of both their imitation of the white man as well as an indication of their willingness to alter themselves so as to live a new kind of life. This spirit of accommodation in Merton's indigenous peoples is never reciprocated by the white culture.

Although there is a brief suspension of the mood of calm by a sardonic reference to Western standards of beauty ("Natural spray dispenser/ A special extract/ For four-eyed ladies of fashion/MY SIN"), the atmosphere is predominantly one of freshness and vitality (*CP*, p. 484):

> Sunrise. New Kingdom.
> Fresh wakes sweet tropic earth!
> Tribute paid in cotton
> For the Four Men
> (North South East West)
> In Chichen. (*CP*, p. 487)

The tribute that the Mayans pay to fertility gods is a mild and gracious acknowledgment of their dependence on nature and is distinguished from the tribute that they will later pay in blood and in the sacrifice of their culture to the Spaniards.

Darkness overtakes this section of the poem because of famine and the degeneration of the Mayan mythdream, an inevitability in Merton's cyclical view of culture. The days of the honey-offering are replaced by inner dissension and by raids from the warlike Toltecs. Amidst the upheaval the stabilizing mythology and arts of the Mayans gradually vanish:

> Strangled is the flute-hero the painter
> Yaxal Chuen the jeweler
> The Ape Ixkanyultu "Precious Voice"
> His throat is now cut gods driven out
> Singers scattered. (*CP*, p. 490)

Decay follows: "Little by little/ We are degraded/ Wives of our aristocrats/Take money/ To sleep with enemies" (*CP*, p. 493). Eventually, there is the intrusion of the Spanish conquerors, whose heavy boots are ironically as welcome as they are frightening to the despairing Mayans. Merton's view becomes sardonic here, like that of the great Mexican muralist Diego Rivera, who painted similar scenes of the conquest:

Arrival of the turkey cocks
Strutting and gobbling
Redneck captains with whips
Fire in their fingers
Worse than Itzaes
Friars behind every rock every tree
Doing business
Bargaining for our souls
Book burners and hangmen. (*CP*, p. 493)

The culture of the Mayans was thus extinguished, and Merton uses the cycle of their rise and fall from innocence to darkness as a powerful archetypal symbol by which the development of other cultures in *The Geography of Lograire* can be measured.

In line with the prevailing contrapuntal technique the "South" section of the poem is followed immediately by "North." This polarizing allows the qualities of each of the two geographical, cultural, and psychic worlds to appear in sharp relief. In terms of Merton's personal geography "North" is where he came from. Thus, this section deals initially with New York and London, the scenes of his childhood and adolescence, which although sometimes dimly remembered were always a deep part of him—"Forgotten world/All along/ Dream places/ Words in my feet" (*CP*, p. 497). The New York setting encompasses not only scenes from his early upbringing, but also symbolizes America's industrial wasteland: "A land of sandpits here without a single mountain" (*CP*, p. 501).

In the preface Merton described "Queen's Tunnel" as the most subjective part of the poem, thereby accounting for its surrealistic, stream-of-consciousness style, a style that appears to have been inspired in part by his readings on shamanism.[62] He characterized his method in this section as consisting of free-flowing, unconscious images mixed with real places and events, adding that the imagery was deliberately compressed and that it was meant to be only "half-penetrable."[63] "Queen's Tunnel" is set amidst freight yards, the Brooklyn crematory, and the tunnel under the East River that led into Manhattan. The crematory became the basis of the funnel house symbol that hangs over the section, a place that had a literal significance for Merton since his mother and grandparents had been cremated there.

The section represents the point in *The Geography of Lograire* where Merton came closest to acknowledging the link with Villon that had been embedded in the title of the poem. "Queen's Tunnel" was his *Grand Testament* — his fantasia on love and death, Eros and Thanatos — the motif that underlies the structure of this part of the poem. He handles the sexual motif with aplomb, as in his depiction of adolescent sexuality: "Several called Frank went all the way" (*CP*, p. 503). In general the Eros and Thanatos pattern is conveyed through a stimulating sequence involving a streaming of social and personal as well as conscious and subconscious elements:

Sleepy time under the thickest summers.
Insect lights and swings. Mortal tinkle
of porches and glasses . . . It was light
week in Lograire and all the phones. I am
back from Curaçao she said. (They have
wires in their voices when they want in
Lograire.) When they want you should come
by train to the tunnels. (*CP*, pp. 501-502)

The method is cumulative. The summer season ("light week") provides a natural backdrop for both the voice of the woman and the stirrings of passion. The setting is Gothically overshadowed by macabre tunnels that are projected as the outcome of lust and by the demonic funnel house that watches with "pointed eyes" (*CP*, p. 501). Adding to the complexity of the scene, the young Merton finds himself diverted from the throb of sexuality by the call of the dead, a summons that eventually comes from every member of his family: "I cannot come," he tells a lover, "I have dead people to attend to" (*CP*, p. 502). The drive of sexuality has become part of his memory of death, just as death in turn has circumscribed his awakening passion. The effect is not a simple opposition of the pull of life and death since sexuality is itself linked with death and, through the imagery of the wires, with the subhuman dynamism that has overtaken the whole society. Thus, New York, Merton's electronic Babylon, metaphorically resembles the woman whose voice is carried seductively over the wires; New York is itself a "singing telephone" (CP, p. 505).

Scenes of Merton's adolescent passion are effectively superimposed on the general American sexual malaise, which has been brought about by the specious mythdreams of the media: "Change the flame to number eight. Dreamy glass box will benefit the same. He sleeps wailing for a mate" (CP, p. 509). Merton was not opposed to sexuality, but rather to the perversion of it that seemed to be part of America's heritage. The English Ranters of the seventeenth century are used to illustrate this theme. The Ranters were religious enthusiasts, who preached the essential goodness and divinity of all life—including sexuality. Although popular with the poor, the Ranters were persecuted and eventually suppressed by the established Church, which in that period of English history was Puritan. The mythdream of the Ranters was a mirror opposite of the repressive code of the Puritans. In this way they resemble other groups visited in *The Geography of Lograire*, groups that symbolize the subconscious needs of societies that, like those of individuals, inevitably and abrasively assert themselves.

The Ranters believed that there would be a "generall Restauration wherein all men shall be reconciled to God and saved," a proposition that met with a perfunctory reaction from the established Church: "Impious doctrine" (CP, p. 520). The section is given immediacy through Merton's discriminating choice of historical texts, such as that in which the Ranter Jacob Bauthemly articulates his vision:

"Nay, I see that God is in all creatures,
Man and Beast, Fish and Fowle,
And every green thing from the highest cedar to the
    ivey on the wall;
And that God is the life and being of them all . . .
Sin is the dark side of God but God is not
    the author of sin." (CP, pp. 522-523)

If the suppression of the Ranters was inevitable in the seventeenth century, Merton felt that such a doctrine would be a thorn in the side of many orthodox believers even now. His support for the Ranters' faith in the salvation of all men is echoed in his poem "Origen" (1966). Origen's merciful prophecy that hell was a temporary state and that the damned would eventually repent was received reproachfully by the medieval Church. However, the Church came around to an acceptance of the

> . . . sweet poison
> Of compassion in this man
> Who thought he heard all beings
> From stars to stones, angels to elements, alive
> Crying for the Redeemer with a live grief.[64]

Following the general pattern of placing civilized societies next to primitive ones, Merton included in "North" a section on the Arctic wilderness. His source was the *Journal of the Kane Relief Expedition* by Dr. James Laws which he had come across in *Polar Notes,* a journal published by the Dartmouth College Library. [65] A superb diarist himself, he plunged into the record of the 1855 expedition that had set out in search of Edward Kane, explorer and rugged individualist, whom he perceived as fleeing the failure of the new world, a failure that grasping nineteenth century enterprise had made evident.

A critic of the poem, James York Glimm, has interpreted Kane as carrying into the Arctic wilderness the same infectious spirit of exploitation that marred his civilization: "His self-awareness shrunk to zero, Kane dutifully subdues, then catalogues new regions, and finally moves on."[66] Glimm missed one of the essential truths about Merton's characterization of Kane. Whatever the initial reason for his exploration, Kane is hypnotized by the savage Arctic beauty that envelops him. Instead of leaving the conspicuous markers of his progress that he was supposed to leave, he leaves only:

> A small mound
> A homeopathic vial containing a mosquito

Covered with cotton
A small piece of cartridge paper
With the letters "OK" written on it
As if with the point of a bullet. (*CP*, p. 530)

This is the action of a man who has come to despise detail and whose attention is focused on depths elsewhere.

Ironically, Dr. Laws, whose diary furnishes this section with its principal materials, thrives on detail and is eminently a creature of his acquisitive civilization. His account is filled with carefully considered observations, but these observations reveal that he does not value the Arctic Eden into which as a civilized man he has been privileged to come. His early perceptions are promising:

> Quiet mountains green and
> Silver Edens
> Walls of an
> Empty country. (*CP*, p. 525)

His subsequent perceptions become sullied, however, by hackneyed imagery that obscures the immaculate originality of his Arctic surroundings: "One iceberg on our port bow/ Resembled a lady dressed in white/ Before her shrine" (*CP*, p. 525).

The natural harmony of the Arctic is felt ("whales came/ And played around us all day"), but the pristine significance of the Arctic wilderness in contrast with the rest of the North American continent is not recognized by the well-intentioned doctor. Similarly, he fails to see the meaning of the awesome scale of nature in relation to man, even when that meaning is thrust at him:

> A crack in the cliff
> Ninety yards wide
> Secret basin land —
> Locked dark
> All stone straight up
> Two thousand feet

Into the rain
Not a spot of green
I inquir'd where to
Look for the town
He pointed to
Twelve cabins. (*CP*, pp. 526-527)

The precariousness of man's tenure in the Arctic which Merton saw as a paradigm of all life is symbolized memorably in the obscure graveyard perched high on a wet cliff, where bodies "sleep in crevices/ Covered with light earth then stones" *CP*, p. 527). The sighting of the hamlet is a good example of Merton's handling of his sources. In the *Journal of the Kane Relief Expedition* the scene unfolded as follows:

On all sides the mountains rose up to the height of 2000 feet, not a green spot could be seen, all was black, dreary & desolate. I enquired of Lovell 'where to look for the town.' He pointed to a small knot of houses, some 10 or 12 in number, with a few Esquimaux huts scattered here and there along the sides of the mountains.[67]

A comparison of this passage with the extract from *The Geography of Logaire* given earlier illustrates that Merton made the scene taut and firm, ridding the source passage of its diffusion through careful selectivity and through rearrangement of the details into compressed rhythmic units. One notices specifically that he chose not to use Dr. Laws's image of the "knot" of houses, but opted for the more prosaic "Twelve cabins." The knot image would have placed the houses together and given the impression of solidarity even if on a small scale. Merton's phrasing makes it appear that the cabins are arranged randomly and that each must stand alone against the elements, thereby sharpening his focus on the power of nature and the vulnerability of man. In addition, he did not place quotation marks around the passage because he wanted to emphasize the scene rather than the narrator. He generally used quotation marks to throw an ironic light on his speakers. Thus it can be seen that he altered his sources quite liberally in order to suit his purpose.

Dr. Laws fails to learn from the Eskimo people with whom he comes into contact. "They do not understand/ Time, "he observes patronizingly, by which he means the clock time of his civilization (*CP*, p. 532). Merton portrays Dr. Laws as having a camera mind that does not appreciate the significance of what it observes:

> "I would have given almost anything for a daguerrotype of that room. Voices soft and clear eyes light blue or hazel. Not one bad tooth. Their hair is all combed up to the top of the head and twisted into a knot and tied with ribbons, red for the unmarried, blue for the married ones. Jumper or jacket lined with finely dressed deerskin trimmed with fur and a band of ribbon. The most beautiful part of their dress is the pantaloons of spotted seal, very soft, with an embroidered stripe down the front which says: 'ready for marriage.' "(*CP*, p. 528)

Laws's timidly voyeuristic approach to the Eskimo women is typical of his approach to the wilderness. Beneath his deference is the instinct of the exploiter, a trait that becomes abruptly evident in a small incident that Merton includes almost parenthetically in the sequence:

> "We entered a cave at the foot of the cliff and found it filled with young loons and gulls.
>
> So we shot 500 weighing 1172 lbs." (*CP*, p. 533)

In thus focusing on the blind acquisitiveness of Northern man and in prefiguring the rape of the last remaining wilderness, Merton placed himself more firmly than ever within the thematic mainstream of American literature.

"East" begins with a breathtaking journey through Africa and Asia under the guidance of Ibn Battuta, a fourteenth century

Moroccan Moslem, whose epic travels carried him to the Pacific. From that point Merton pushes out into the islands of the Pacific with the sequence on cargo cults, preparatory to coming to rest in America in the last section — "West."

Juxtaposed with the tension and aggressiveness of the Kane expedition, the Moslem mythdream seems mild and sensuous — at least at first:

> Cloisters (khanqahs) of Darvishes
> Built by aristocrats
> Have silver rings on their doors
> The mystics sit down to eat
> Each from his private bowl. (CP, p. 538)

Merton became interested in Moslem spirituality during the 1960s, and his judgments of it are represented in this section. If he felt the beauty of Islam, he was also aware of the ferocity that lay embedded in Moslem history: "Twenty thousand heretics/ Were slaughtered. The rest hid in the mountains" (CP, p. 541).

The civilized world is represented in "East" primarily by the anthropologist Bronislaw Malinowski, whose *Diary in the Strict Sense of the Term* (1967) Merton used as a symbol of the white man's experience of cultural shock. Malinowski's experience serves as a foil to the sections of the sequence that portray the shock to primitive societies brought about by the encroachment of the white man. The cultural shock that Malinowski experiences is due in part to his inability to do without amenities of Western civilization:

> at night (low tide)
> "I urinated from a height of 13 feet."
> Morning again gentle hills
> Sprawling spidery trees.
> "I evacuated straight into the sea
> From a privy above the water." (CP, p. 546)

Merton's portrayal of Malinowski suggests that the modern anthropologist ran the risk of continuing the colonial attitudes of an earlier period. The following blunt entry from Malinowski's diary makes this evident: "I gave them portions of tobacco and they all walked away without posing long enough for a time exposure. My feelings toward them: exterminate the brutes" (*CP*, p. 551).

The poems about the cargo cult of the South Sea islands follow. If Merton relied on a number of anthropological studies for this section, the most important of which are listed in the notes appended to the poem, he felt that he was at least original in dealing with the cargo cult in such a way that it became a universal symbol of human unrest and of man's attempt to cope with the problems of rapid change. The cargo cult was an ingenuous Messianic movement among certain native groups of the Pacific islands that focused on obtaining cargo or worldly goods in order to gain the sort of power and prestige that the islanders associated with the white men who had colonized their lands. The islanders attributed the white man's exalted status to the shipments of cargo by ship or plane that seemed to materialize out of nowhere. The cult was thus an unconscious parody of Western culture. Inevitably, when the cargo did not arrive, the cult broke up, but Merton was impressed with the fact that disappearing cults were followed by a succession of new ones. In this connection, in an unpublished manuscript entitled "Cargo Theology" he wrote that all men had a need to be "constantly readjusting, reshaping, putting together in a new form" the basic symbols of their mythdream.[68] Although Western man regarded phenomena like the cargo cults with skepticism at best, Merton felt that the drive for recognition and satisfaction that underlay these cults was universal and poignant.

In spite of his sympathy for those who had formed cargo cults, Merton maintained the urbanity of his overall approach in *The Geography of Lograire* in describing the cult. An example is his droll description of the attempt by cult members to negotiate with the god of cargo so that precious freight might be diverted their way:

The ancestors are alive and well in the sky immediately above Sydney Australia . . . Plenty for everybody, black

and white alike. While the Cargo is at sea the white crew
spends all its time changing the labels and readdressing
the natives' shipments to planters, missionaries, government officials and policemen. The problem now is
how to get Cargo direct without recourse to ships and
planes belonging to white men? (CP, p. 559)

The apocalyptic character of the cult encouraged the destruction of all attachments, which unfortunately included the
sacrifice of older and often superior rituals. Inevitably, cult
members awakened to the fact that they had been culturally
sterilized through their contacts with the white man and they
turned to violence — as in the poem about the white colonizer,
Mr. Clapcott, to whom the cult sent the following arresting
message: "Five special delivery bullets in the chest tomorrow"
(CP, p. 569). The hope expressed in the poem that the killing of
Clapcott would bring cargo from America acts as a transition to
the final section of The Geography of Lograire.
   "West" brings the book full circle, completing Merton's cir-
cumnavigation of the world. With his bent toward science Western man liked to deny, Merton believed, that he was guided by
any sort of mythdream. "Myth Number One for us," he wrote in
the treatise on cargo theology, is that "we have no myths."[69] He
had already documented the West's garish mythdream in Cables
to the Ace. In The Geography of Lograire he focused on the decay of
that dream, especially in "Day Six O'Hare Telephane." The poem
was based on his flight from Louisville to San Francisco in the
spring of 1968, which included a stopover at Chicago's O'Hare
airport. Crisp descriptions of aircraft are interwoven with Hindu
sayings in order to accent the shallowness of the West's
mythdream with its glorification of the airplane—the epitome of
Western technology:

Comes a big slow fish with tailfins erect in light smog
And one other leaves earth
Go trains of insect machines
Thirtynine generals signal eight
Contact barrier four

A United leaves earth
Square silver bug moves into shade under wing building.
(CP, p. 575)

The flight is marked by programmed friendliness from the pilot
and crew. The pilot has a "savage muffled voice/ With playboy
accents," while the stewardesses are pretty doll people — "mi-
gnonnes" (CP, p. 581)

Emphasizing objectivity and realism, Merton focuses on a
self-assertive black passenger, his pockets stuffed with food
stamps, who is pictured outside the "highest toilet in the world/
To establish a record in rights" (CP, p. 580). Power is what makes
America run, the poem suggests, and the black passenger is
simply reflecting his nationality rather than his race:

> High above the torment
> Of milling wind and storms
> We are all High Police Thors
> Holding our own weapons
> Into the milk mist each alone
> As our battering ram
> Fires us all into Franciscan West. (CP, pp. 580-581)

The motif of cultural shock is expressed in "West" through the
portrayal of the ghost dance religion of the American plains'
Indians of the nineteenth century. The subject provides an effective transition since it involves the area of the Dakotas that
Merton had flown over in "Day Six O'Hare Telephane." The
ghost dance movement was similar to the cargo cults of the South
Pacific, except that instead of cargo the Indians concentrated on
ritualistic dancing to throw off the yoke of the white man and
claim his accumulated treasures for themselves. The cult did not
gravitate toward violence. One hope the Indians had was for an
idyllic integration with a white society in which they would be
treated as equals.

The group spread and was inevitably suppressed by a suspicious white America. The mythdream had already shown signs
of degeneration, though, and Merton's dramatization of the In-

dians skillfully brings out the pathos of their situation:

> Dr. George came to the mouth of Lost River where he found Captain Jack and the people. He came in winter when no grass was growing. He said that when the grass was eight inches high the dead would return. The deer and all the animals would return. "The whites will burn up and vanish without leaving any ashes. Dance or you will be turned to stone."
> Then everybody danced and jumped in the river. They came out of the water with ice in their hair. (CP, pp. 590-591)

Merton's geographical and historical cycles point repeatedly to the same truth. Man's deepest needs have not been met by his experiments in culture, and this failure has been especially evident in the West — where the material world has been most successfully brought under control.

The Geography of Lograire was Merton's way of coming to terms with recent developments in American poetry. Earlier, he had avoided the forms used by recent American poets because he associated these forms with sterile experimentation. He searched for new forms in the 1950s, but he was limited by the fact that as far as poetic theory was concerned he was working in a vacuum. His position was especially unfortunate since his talent lay in the imaginative way in which he reacted to other people's ideas. By the 1960s he had convinced himself that the use of open forms in contemporary poetry with their idiosyncratic variations in line, image, and rhythm could be harnessed to carry the weight ·of his teeming social and spiritual themes. Cables to the Ace represented his first major attempt to bring all of these elements together. In Cables he experimented with the lyric/epic format that was to reach consummate expression in The Geography of Lograire.

Apart from being a fresh sign of Merton's increasing mastery of poetic form, The Geography of Lograire led to his being recognized as an important figure in recent American poetry. The range of his work strikes one in retrospect as impressive — from the austerely beautiful religious lyrics of the early period to the inventiveness and structural complexity of the later style. In the late 1960s he had finally come to feel that the poet and the contemplative in him were one, and this confidence gives the later poems an attractive energy and buoyancy that seem in hindsight to have been full of promise.

Notes

[1]W. S. Merwin, "Urbanity and Grace," *New York Times Book Review* (May 26, 1957), p. 28.

[2]*A Controversy of Poets,* ed. Paris Leary and Robert Kelly (New York, 1965).

[3]Tape #233-B (Feb. 13, 1966). Lecture on post-World War II poets.

[4]*Conjectures of a Guilty Bystander,* p. 119.

[5]"Paradise Bugged," *The Critic,* XXV (1967), p. 70.

[6]"A Catch of Anti-Letters," *Voyages,* XI (1968), p. 52.

[7]Notebook #63 (1956).

[8]Tape #199-A (Jan. 29, 1965). Lecture on poetry.

[9]*Early Poems: 1940-42* (Lexington, Ky., 1971).

[10]*The Seven Storey Mountain,* p. 236.

[11]Ibid., p. 304.

[12]The letter was sent by Brother Campion, who indicated he was acting on Merton's behalf, to Sister Rosemarie Gavin, San Rafael, Calif., July 7, 1951.

[13]Robert Lowell, "The Verses of Thomas Merton," *Commonweal,* XLII (June 22, 1945), p. 240.

[14]Letter by Merton to the Catholic Poetry Society of America *Bulletin,* IV (1041), p. 10.

[15]*Thirty Poems* (Norfolk, Conn., 1944). Reprinted in *The Collected Poems of Thomas Merton* (New York, 1977) pp. 51-52. Further references will be to this edition and will be incorporated in the text. Regarding the composition of these poems, see my article "The Ordering of Thomas Merton's Early Poems," Resources for American Literary Study, VIII (1979), pp. 115-117.

[16]*Secular Journal,* p. 161.

[17]*The Seven Storey Mountain,* p. 314.

[18]Letter to Martha Gisi, May 19, 1966.

[19]*A Man in the Divided Sea* (Norfolk, Conn., 1946). Reprinted in the *Collected Poems,* p. 61. Further references will be to this edition and

will be incorporated in the text.

[20]*The Seven Storey Mountain*, p. 11.

[21]*Seeds of Destruction*, p. 299.

[22]*Figures for an Apocalypse* (New York, 1947). Reprinted in the *Collected Poems*, p. 152. Subsequent references will be to this edition and will be incorporated in the text.

[23]*The Tears of the Blind Lions* (New York, 1949). Reprinted in the *Collected Poems*, p. 220. Subsequent references will be to this edition and will be incorporated in the text.

[24]Letter to Mark Van Doren, July 30, 1956.

[25]James Dickey, "In the Presence of Anthologies," *Sewanee Review*, LXVI (1958), pp. 294-314.

[26]Donald Hall, "Sincerity and the Muse," *Saturday Review*, XL (July 6, 1957), p. 30.

[27]*Sign of Jonas*, p. 270.

[28]*The Strange Islands* (New York, 1957). Reprinted in the *Collected Poems*, p. 283. Subsequent references will be to this edition and will be incorporated in the text.

[29]"First Lesson about Man," *Saturday Review*, LII (Jan. 11, 1969), p. 21. Reprinted in the *Collected Poems*, p. 626.

[30]Preface to *The Strange Islands*. Unpaginated.

[31]Mark Van Doren, "Introduction," *The Selected Poems of Thomas Merton* (New York, 1959), p. xi.

[32]*Sign of Jonas*, p. 224.

[33]Sister Thérèse Lentfoehr, "The Solitary," in *Thomas Merton, Monk*, ed. Brother Patrick Hart (New York, 1974), p. 65.

[34]*Emblems of a Season of Fury* (New York, 1963). Reprinted in the *Collected Poems*, p. 316. Subsequent references will be to this edition and will be incorporated in the text.

[35]"Introduction," *Wisdom of the Desert: Sayings from the Desert Fathers of the Fourth Century* (New York, 1960), p. 11.

[36]Letter to Barbara Hubbard, Feb. 16, 1968.

[37]"The Time of the End is the Time of No Room," in *Raids on the Unspeakable*, p. 73.

[38]Letter to Pheme Perkins, May 12, 1967.

[39]"Letters in a Time of Crisis," in *Seeds of Destruction*, p. 292.

[40]"For the Spanish Poet Miguel Hernandez," *Sewanee Review*, LXXIV (1966), pp. 897-898. Reprinted in the *Collected Poems*, pp. 641-642.

[41]"With the World in My Bloodstream," *Florida Quarterly*, I (1967), pp. 19-21. Reprinted in the *Collected Poems*, p. 616.

[42]Notebook #79 (1966).

[43]*Asian Journal*, p. 286.

[44]"War and the Crisis of Language," in *The Critique of War: Contemporary Philosophical Explorations*, ed. Robert Ginsberg (Chicago, 1969), p. 119.

[45]"Why Alienation is for Everybody," in "Collected Essays," vol. 2, p. 29. Manuscript.

[46]See Miller Williams, "Introduction," *Poems and Antipoems* (New York, 1967), p. vii.

[47]Nicanor Parra, "Young Poets," in *Poems and Antipoems*, p. 143.

[48]*Asian Journal*, p. 118.

[49]*Cables to the Ace* (New York, 1968). Reprinted in the *Collected Poems*, p. 403. Subsequent references will be to this edition and will be incorporated in the text.

[50]"Blake and the New Theology," *Sewanee Review*, LXXVI (1968), p. 679.

[51]Letter to W. H. Ferry, Sept. 17, 1966.

[52]Letter to W. H. Ferry, Oct. 4, 1966.

[53]Letter to Dr. June Yungblut, March 6, 1968.

[54]Letter to Robert Lax, Nov. 4, 1966.

[55]Letter to James Laughlin, June 4, 1967.

[56]Jascha Kessler, "Keys to Ourselves," *Saturday Review*, XIII (1970), p. 34.

[57]Letter to James Laughlin, April 18, 1967.

[58]Letter to W. H. Ferry, Sept. 24, 1967.

[59]Letter to Dorothy Emmett, Oct. 16, 1967.

[60]"Author's Note," *The Geography of Lograire* (New York, 1969). Reprinted in the *Collected Poems*, p. 457. Subsequent references will be to this edition and will be incorporated in the text.

[61]Notebook #81. The entry is dated Dec. 25, 1966.

[62]This is the opinion of Louisville poet, Ronald Seitz, who visited Merton while he was writing *Geography of Lograire*.

[63]"Why Alienation is for Everybody," p. 29.

[64]"Origen" was published in *New Directions in Prose and Poetry*, XIX, ed. James Laughlin (New York, 1966), pp. 288-289. Reprinted in the *Collected Poems*, p. 641.

[65]"Dr. James Laws' Journal of the Kane Relief Expedition of 1855," *Polar Notes*, no. 7 (1967), pp. 1-24.

[66]James York Glimm, "Thomas Merton's Last Poem: *The Geography of Lograire*," *Renascence*, XXVI (1974), p. 99.

[67]"Dr. James Laws' Journal of the Kane Relief Expedition of 1855," p. 8.

[68]"Cargo Theology," pp. 14-15. Manuscript.

[69]"Cargo Theology," p. 6.

A Final Approach

IN THE LIGHT OF THOMAS MERTON'S primary allegiance to a vocation other than art, one feels somewhat perplexed by his prodigious publication. In spite of some early scruples, however, he came to accept the artist in himself as a viable agent of the contemplative life. Furthermore, he used different art forms to meet the demands of what developed into a fairly complex way of life.

He used the essay, for example, as the vehicle for his working life — the public voice. As an essayist he evolved from a severely traditional awareness of his public role to a lively reformism that allowed him to develop a suggestive, imagistic style and to move from the ecclesiastical platitudes of books like *Silence in Heaven* (1956) to the impassioned tone and symbolistic mode of *Raids on the Unspeakable* (1966).

The journals convey Merton's private and most personal voice. Even though written with the understanding, as was true of everything he wrote, that they might be published, they reveal his sensitivity to the candor and improvisation that are implicit in the form. The diaries reflect a bright surface in which are found the minutiae of his daily consciousness, the strain and the moments of blissful release, the freshness of the natural world and the mind embattled, endlessly it sometimes seems, against both the ponderous and the trite. *The Sign of Jonas* is the strongest of Merton's published journals and is one of the most eloquent books of its kind since Thoreau.

The least persistent form of Merton's art was that of the narrative. Undoubtedly because of his early disappointments in trying to publish his novels, he did not pursue the form after the 1940s. Although *My Argument with the Gestapo* finally appeared in the late 1960s, Merton was again aware of an air of reluctance surrounding its publication, and there is no indication in his notebooks that he intended to take up narrative writing again. Nevertheless, his narrative writing has much to recommend it, and *The Seven Storey Mountain*, already recognized as a spiritual classic, is a formidable example of the storyteller's art.

Feeling increasingly that poetry especially was his way as a contemplative, Merton gave himself to this kind of writing with a vigorous sense of commitment as the years went by. The early poetry — from *Thirty Poems* (1944) to *The Tears of the Blind Lions* (1949) — tends to be anchored in formal, traditional technique and in conventional religious themes, although some of the poems — such as the "Song for Our Lady of Cobre" and "The Reader" — have a lyrical purity that has caused many of Merton's readers to value the early poetry more highly than the later work. The later work is broader in its themes, more technically complex and innovative, and more ambitious in its handling of broad structures. Largely addressing itself to contemporary social themes, the later poetry enters the mainstream of American verse.

Poetry became for Merton a free, associational medium that carried the tide of those creative ideas and that became his principal arena for experimenting with language. In between the tight formalism of the early work and the fluidity of the later poems, the poetry became uneven, notably in volumes like *The Strange Islands.* However, as he searched in the 1950s for a new idiom, he ironically produced some of his finest traditional verse, the "Elegy for the Monastery Barn" being a well-known example. The tendency toward experimentation, however, finally bore fruit in the publication of *The Geography of Lograire.* *The Geography of Lograire* is a distinguished poem, and its appearance in the thick of Merton's career makes his accidental death in Thailand especially unfortunate, not only in terms of his own accomplishment but in the wider context of contemporary literature. As a poet there is no doubt that he had not yet reached his full stride when he was cut down by death in 1968. Nevertheless, his writings, whether in poetry or prose, have a beautiful fullness and integrity. In the case of books like *The Seven Storey Mountain, The Geography of Lograire,* and *The Sign of Jonas,* he reached heights that will secure his place in twentieth century letters for some time to come.

As contemplative and artist Merton's essential insight about contemporary man concerns the value of solitude. Setting himself against the grain of a culture in which solitude was viewed as a sign of neurosis and alienation, he reversed this conventional picture by showing that these effects were more likely to be observed in group man. At first sight his writings would appear to be an anomaly in terms of the social and intellectual temper of his time. However, as is reflected in the popularity of his writings and the breadth of his appeal, he reached those hidden springs in all men whose existence he felt it crucial to expose. With energy and consistency he committed himself to assuaging the frustration of this hidden self and encouraging its deep, unconscious purposes.

Selective Bibliography

Books by Thomas Merton

Albert Camus' 'The Plague': Introduction and Commentary. New York: Seabury Press, 1968.

The Ascent to Truth. New York: Harcourt, Brace, and Co., 1957.

The Asian Journal of Thomas Merton, ed. Naomi Burton, Brother Patrick Hart, James Laughlin, and Amiya Chakravarty. New York: New Directions, 1973.

The Behaviour of Titans. New York: New Directions, 1973.

Bread in the Wilderness. New York: New Directions, 1953.

Cables to the Ace. New York: New Directions, 1968.

The Climate of Monastic Prayer. Spencer, Mass.: Cistercian Publications, 1969.

The Collected Poems of Thomas Merton. New York: New Directions, 1977.

Conjectures of a Guilty Bystander. New York: Doubleday and Co., 1966.

Comtemplation in a World of Action. New York: Doubleday and Co., 1965.

Disputed Questions. New York: Farrar, Straus and Cudahy, 1960.

Early Poems 1940-42. Lexington, Kentucky: Anvil Press Publications, 1971.

Emblems of a Season of Fury. New York: New Directions, 1973.

Faith and Violence. Notre Dame, Indiana: University of Notre Dame Press, 1969.

Figures for an Apocalypse. New York: New Directions, 1948.

Gandhi on Non-Violence, ed. Thomas Merton. New York: New Directions, 1965.

The Geography of Lograire. New York: New Directions, 1969.

The Living Bread. New York: Farrar, Straus and Cudahy, 1956.

A Man in the Divided Sea. Norfolk, Conn.: New Directions, 1947.

Monastic Peace. Trappist, Kentucky: Abbey of Our Lady of Gethsemani, 1958.

My Argument with the Gestapo: A Macaronic Journal. New York:

Doubleday and Co., 1969.

Mystics and Zen Masters. New York: Farrar, Straus and Giroux, 1967.

The New Man. New York: Farrar, Straus and Cudahy, 1961.

New Seeds of Contemplation. New York: New Directions, 1961.

No Man is an Island. New York: Harcourt, Brace, and Co., 1955.

Opening the Bible. Collegeville, Minnesota: Liturgical Press, 1970.

The Original Child Bomb: Points for Meditation to be Scratched on the Walls of a Cave. New York: New Directions, 1962.

Raids on the Unspeakable. New York: New Directions, 1966.

Redeeming the Time. London: Burns and Oates, 1966.

Seasons of Celebration. New York: Farrar, Straus and Cudahy, 1959.

The Secular Journal of Thomas Merton. New York: Farrar, Straus and Cudahy, 1959.

Seeds of Contemplation. Norfolk, Conn.: New Directions, 1949.

Seeds of Destruction. New York: Farrar, Straus and Giroux, 1964.

The Seven Storey Mountain. New York: Harcourt, Brace, and Co., 1949.

The Sign of Jonas. New York: Harcourt, Brace, and Co., 1953.

The Strange Islands. New York: New Directions, 1957.

The Tears of the Blind Lions. New York: New Directions, 1949.

Thirty Poems. Norfolk, Conn.: New Directions, 1944.

Thomas Merton: The Monastic Journey. Edited by Brother Patrick Hart. Mission, Kansas: Sheed, Andrews and McNeel, Inc., 1977.

Thoughts in Solitude. New York: Farrar, Straus and Cudahy, 1958.

The Waters of Siloe. New York: Harcourt, Brace, and Co., 1949.

The Wisdom of the Desert. New York: New Directions, 1960.

Zen and the Birds of Appetite. New York: New Directions, 1968.

Articles by Thomas Merton

"Advice to a Young Prophet." *Catholic Worker,* XXVIII (Jan., 1962), 4.

"Art and Morality." *The New Catholic Encyclopedia.* Wash., D.C., 1967. Vol. I, 864-867.

"Art and Worship." *Sponsa Regis,* XXXI (1959), 114-117.

"Auschwitz: A Family Camp." *Catholic Worker,* XXXIII (Nov., 1967), 4-5.

"'Baptism in the Forest:' Wisdom and Initiation in William Faulkner." *Mansions of the Spirit.* Edited by George Panichas. New York: Hawthorn, 1967, 19-44.

"Blake and the New Theology." *Sewanee Review,* LXXVI (1968), 673-682.

"Camus: Journals of the Plague Years." *Sewanee Review,* LXXV (1967), 717-730.

"Can We Survive Nihilism?" *Saturday Review,* L (April 15, 1967), 16-19.

"A Catch of Anti-Letters." *Voyages XI* (Winter-Spring, 1968), 44-56.

"The Catholic and Creativity: Theology of Creativity." *American Benedictine Review,* XI (1960), 197-213.

"Comments on Dr. Prince's and Dr. Savage's Paper on Mystical States and Regression." *The R. M. Bucke Memorial Society Newsletter,* I (1966), 4-5.

"Day of a Stranger." *Hudson Review,* XX (1967), 211-218.

"Death." *Prophetic Voices: Ideas and Words in Revolution.* Edited by Ned O'Gorman. New York: Random House, 1969, 230-238.

"Ishi: A Meditation." *Catholic Worker,* XXXIII (March, 1967), 5-6.

"News of the Joyce Industry." *Sewanee Review,* LXXVII (1969), 543-554.

"Notes on Sacred and Profane Art." *Jubilee,* IV (1956), 25-32.

"Nuclear War and Christian Responsibility." *Commonweal,* LXXV (Feb. 9, 1962), 509-513.

"The Other Side of Despair: Christian Existentialism." *Critic,* XXIV (1965), 12-33.

"Paradise Bugged." *Critic,* XXV (1967), 69-71.

"Poetry and Contemplation: A Reappraisal." *Commonweal,* LXIX (Oct. 24, 1958), 87-92.

"Poetry and the Contemplative Life." *Commonweal,* XLVI (July 4, 1947), 280-286.

"Rafael Alberti and His Angels." *Continuum,* V (1967), 175-179.

"Sacred Art and the Spiritual Life." *Sponsa Regis,* XXXI (1960), 133-140.

"The Sacred City." *The Center Magazine,* I (March, 1968), 72-77.
"The Self of Modern Man and the New Christian Conscious-
ness." *The R.M. Bucke Memorial Society Newsletter,* II (1967),
17-21.
"The Stranger: Poverty of an Anti-Hero." *Unicorn Journal,* II
(1968), 10-19.
"The Street is for Celebration." *The Mediator,* XX (1969), 2-4.
"Symbolism: Communication or Communion?" *Monastic Ex-
change,* II (1970), 1-10.
"Terror and the Absurd: Violence and Nonviolence in Albert
Camus." *Motive,* XXIX (1969), 5-15.
"Todo Y Nada: Writing and Contemplation," *Renascence,* II
(1950), 87-101.
"The True Legendary Sound: The Poetry and Criticism of Edwin
Muir." *Sewanee Review,* LXXV (1967), 317-324.
"War and Vision." *Catholic Worker,* XXXIII (December, 1967), 4.
"War and the Crisis of Language." *The Critique of War: Contem-
porary Philosophical Explorations.* Edited by Robert Ginsberg.
Chicago, 1969, 99-119.
"The Wild Places." *The Center Magazine,* I (July, 1968), 40-44.
"Wilderness and Paradise." *Cistercian Studies,* II (1967), 83-89.
"Wisdom in Emptiness." *New Directions in Prose and Poetry.*
Edited by James Laughlin. New York: New Directions, 1961.
Vol. XVII, 65-101.
"William Congdon." *Liturgical Arts,* XXX (February, 1962), 60.
"Writing as Temperature." *Sewanee Review,* LXXVII (1969), 534-
542.
"Zukofsky: The Paradise Ear." *Peace News,* (July 28, 1967), 8.

Books about Merton

Bailey, Raymond. *Thomas Merton on Mysticism.* New York:
Doubleday and Co., 1975.
Baker, James T. *Thomas Merton, Social Critic: A Study.* Lexington,
Ky: University Press of Kentucky, 1971.
Breit, Marquita. *Thomas Merton: A Bibliography.* Metchuen, N.J.:
The Scarecrow Press, 1974.
Dell'Isola, Frank. *Thomas Merton: A Bibliography.* Kent, Ohio:

Kent State University Press, 1975.

Griffin, John Howard. *A Hidden Wholeness: The Visual World of Thomas Merton.* Boston: Houghton Mifflin Co., 1970.

Hart, Patrick, ed. *Thomas Merton, Monk: A Monastic Tribute.* New York: Sheed and Ward, Inc., 1974.

Kelly, Frederick J. *Man before God: Thomas Merton on Social Responsibility.* New York: Doubleday and Co., 1974.

Lentfoehr, Sr. Therese. *Words and Silence: On the Poetry of Thomas Merton.* New York: New Directions, 1979.

McInerny, Dennis. *Thomas Merton: The Man and His Work.* Kalamazoo, Michigan: Cistercian Publications, 1974.

Rice, Edward. *The Man in the Sycamore Tree: The Good Times and Hard Life of Thomas Merton.* New York: Doubleday and Co., 1970.

Woodcock, George. *Thomas Merton: Monk and Poet.* New York: Farrar, Straus and Giroux, 1978.

Articles and Dissertations about Merton

Baciu, Stefan. "Latin America and Spain in the Poetic World of Thomas Merton." *Revue de Littérature Comparée,* XLI (1967), 288-300.

Baker, James T. "An Image in the Making: Thomas Merton's Early Interpreters." *Mississippi Valley Collection Bulletin,* (Fall, 1972), 20-28.

_____."The Two Cities of Thomas Merton." *Catholic World,* CCXI (July, 1970), 151-155.

Bogan, Louise. "Verse." *New Yorker,* XXII (Oct. 5, 1946), 113-115.

Boyd, John D. "Christian Imaginative Patterns and the Poetry of Thomas Merton." *Greyfriar-Siena Studies in Literature,* XIII (1972), 3-14.

Browning, Mary Carmel. "Father Thomas Louis Merton: The Trappist Poet of Contemplation." *Kentucky Authors: A History of Kentucky Literature.* Evansville, Indiana: Keller-Crescent Co., 1968, 214-222.

Burton-Stone, Naomi. "Thomas Merton's Mountain." *More Than Sentinels.* New York: Doubleday and Co., 1964, 46-50.

Davidson, Eugene. "Poet's Shelf." *Yale Review,* XXXVII (1948), 745-750.

Dickey, James. "In the Presence of Anthologies." *Sewanee Review,* LXVI (1958), 294-314.

Eberhart, Richard. "Four Poets." *Sewanee Review*, LV (1947), 324-336.

Elmen, Paul. "Already in Custody." *Christian Century*, LXXVI (Oct. 21, 1959), 1215.

Glimm, James York. "Exile Ends in Satire: Thomas Merton's Cables to the Ace." *Cithara* XI (November, 1971), 31-40.

_____"Thomas Merton's Last Poem: *The Geography of Lograire*." *Renascence*, XXVI (1974), 95-104.

Grayston, Donald. "Textual Variation and Theological Development in Thomas Merton's *Seeds of Contemplation* and *New Seeds of Contemplation*. M.A. thesis, University of Toronto, 1974.

Griffin, John Howard. "In Search of Thomas Merton." *Thomas Merton Studies Center*. Santa Barbara, Calif: Unicorn Press. 1971, 17-24.

Hall, Donald. "Sincerity and the Muse." *Saturday Review*, XL (July 6, 1957), 29-30.

Higgins, Michael. "Thomas Merton: The Poet and the Word." *Cistercian Studies*, XII (1977), 292-307.

Irwin, John T. "The Crisis of Regular Form." *Sewanee Review*, LXXXI (1973), 158-171.

Giroux, Robert. "Introduction." *Flannery O'Connor: The Complete Stories*. New York: Farrar, Straus and Giroux, 1971, xiii-xiv.

_____"Thomas Merton: 1915-1968." *Columbia College Today*, XV (Spring, 1969), 69-71.

Johnson, Carol. "The Vision and the Poem." *Poetry*. CXCVI (1960), 387-391.

Justice, Donald. "Sacred and Secular." *Poetry*, XCI (1957), 41-44.

Kelly, Richard. "Thomas Merton and Poetic Vitality." *Renascence*, XII (1960), 139-142, 148.

Kessler, Jascha. "Keys to Ourselves." *Saturday Review*, LIII (May 2, 1970), 34-35, 42-43.

Kilcourse, George. "Incarnation as the Integrating Principle in Thomas Merton's Poetry." Ph.D. thesis, Fordham University, 1974.

Krikorian, Y.H. "The Fruits of Mysticism." *New Republic*, CXXI (Sept. 12, 1949), 245-260.

Kountz, Peter. "The Seven Storey Mountain of Thomas Merton."

Thought, XLIV (1974), 250-267.

Landess, Thomas. "Monastic Life and the Secular City." *Sewanee Review*, LXXV (1969), 530-535.

Lowell, Robert. "The Verses of Thomas Merton." *Commonweal*, XLII (June 22, 1945), 240-242.

McDonnell, Thomas P. "An Interview with Thomas Merton." *Motive*, XXVII (October, 1967), 32-41.

_____"The Poetry of Thomas Merton." *Spirit*, XXV (March, 1958), 23-30.

Merwin, W.S. "Urbanity and Grace." *New York Times Book Review* (May 26, 1957), 28.

Mizener, Arthur. "The Tears of the Blind Lions." *Poetry*, LXXVI (1950), 224-226.

Murray, Michele. "Thomas Merton, the Public Monk." *National Catholic Reporter*, III (Dec. 21, 1966), 9.

Randall, Virginia F. "Contrapuntal Irony and Theme in Thomas Merton's *The Geography of Lograire*." *Renascence*, XXVIII (1976), 191-202.

Schmidt, Gail. "The Poetry of Thomas Merton: An Introduction." Ph.D. dissertation, University of Wisconsin-Madison, 1976.

Steindal-Rast, David. "Recollections of Thomas Merton's Last Days in the West." *Monastic Studies*, VII (1969), 1-10.

Sturm, Ralph. "Thomas Merton: Poet." *American Benedictine Review*, XXII (March, 1971), 1-20.

Sutton, Walter. "Thomas Merton." *American Free Verse*. New York: New Directions, 1973, 198-203.

_____"Thomas Merton and the American Epic Tradition: The Last Poems." *Contemporary Literature*, XIV (1973), 49-57.

Van Doren, Mark. "Thomas Merton." *America*, CXX (Jan. 4, 1969), 21-22.

Index